Make a Splash!

A KID'S GUIDE TO PROTECTING OUR OCEANS, LAKES, RIVERS, & WETLANDS

by **Cathryn Berger Kaye, M.A.,**
with **Philippe Cousteau**
and **EarthEcho International**

free spirit
PUBLISHING®

EARTHECHO
INTERNATIONAL

Library of Congress Cataloging-in-Publication Data
Kaye, Cathryn Berger.
  Make a splash! : a kid's guide to protecting our oceans, lakes, rivers & wetlands / by Cathryn Berger Kaye ; with Philippe Cousteau and EarthEcho International.
    p. cm.
  Includes index.
  ISBN 978-1-57542-417-0 — ISBN 1-57542-417-7 1. Marine ecology—Juvenile literature. 2. Marine pollution—Prevention—Juvenile literature.
3. Environmentalism—Juvenile literature. I. Title.
  QH541.5.S3K42 2012
  577.7—dc23

                                                                                                                2012032120

eBook ISBN: 978-1-57542-651-8

EarthEcho International and its works or products are not affiliated with, nor in any way in support of, The Cousteau Society or any of its works or trademarks.

Reading Level Grades 3–4; Interest Level Ages 8–12; Fountas & Pinnell Guided Reading Level P

Edited by Meg Bratsch and Alison Behnke; Cover design by Tasha Kenyon; Interior design by Michelle Lee Lagerroos; Illustrations by Jackie Stafford

Photo credits: Kids in Action globes: © Irina Afanasova | Dreamstime.com • Soak It Up Sponges: © Chiyacat | Dreamstime.com • page i: © Januar2000 | Dreamstime.com • page iv: © Alptraum | Dreamstime.com • page 1: © Jojobob | Dreamstime.com • page 3: © Oliclimb | Dreamstime.com • page 6: © Michelle Lee Lagerroos • page 8: © Sara Heintzelman, Farallones Marine Sanctuary Association • page 9: © Claire Fackler, NOAA National Marine Sanctuaries • pages 14–15: © Landd09 | Dreamstime.com • page 15: © William C. Johnson / Kansas Geological Survey • page 16: © Daniel Boiteau | Dreamstime.com • page 18: © NASA image by Robert Simmon and Reto Stöckli • page 23: © Ljupco Smokovski | Dreamstime.com • pages 24–25: © Shannon Workman | Dreamstime.com • page 24: © Nataliia Pogrebna | Dreamstime.com • page 25: © John Wollwerth | Dreamstime.com • page 26: © Coplandj | Dreamstime.com • page 28: © Isselee | Dreamstime.com • page 31: © Photoeuphoria | Dreamstime.com • page 32: © istockphoto.com/laflor • page 33: © Viktor Malyuga | Dreamstime.com • pages 34–35: © Michelle Lee Lagerroos • page 36: © Seesea | Dreamstime.com • page 38: © Dragi Stankovic | Dreamstime.com • pages 40–41: © Tupungato | Dreamstime.com • page 40: © Junede | Dreamstime.com • page 41: © Roman Makhmutov | Dreamstime.com • page 43: © Nataliia Dvukhimenna | Dreamstime.com • page 44: © Jason Kasumovic | Dreamstime.com • page 45: © Arenacreative | Dreamstime.com • page 47: © Katie Fuller • page 49: © Michelle Lee Lagerroos • pages 50–51: © Duncan Noakes | Dreamstime.com • pages 52–53: © Epicstock | Dreamstime.com • page 55: Oil: © Stephan Pietzko | Dreamstime.com • page 55: turtle © NOAA; page 55: clams © Carlos Caetano | Dreamstime.com • page 57: © Wimclaes | Dreamstime.com • page 59: © Ian Holland | Dreamstime.com • page 63: © Anthony Hathaway | Dreamstime.com • pages 64–65: © Richard Carey | Dreamstime.com • page 65: healthy coral © Tasha Kenyon • page 66: © Mychadre77 | Dreamstime.com • page 67: © Carrieanne | Dreamstime.com • page 68: © Benjamin Albiach Galan | Dreamstime.com • page 69: © NOAA • page 69: © David Burdick / NOAA • page 71: Copyright © Nancy Boucha • page 73: © Monterey Bay Aquarium • page 75: © Dmitriy Shironosov | Dreamstime.com • pages 76–77: © Bidouze Stéphane | Dreamstime.com • page 79: © Justinplunkett | Dreamstime.com • page 80: © Michelle Lee Lagerroos • page 81: © Meg Bratsch and © Michelle Lee Lagerroos • page 83: © Britvich | Dreamstime.com • pages 84–85: © istockphoto.com/JBryson • page 86: © Monika Wisniewska | Dreamstime.com • page 87: © Stoycho Stoychev | Dreamstime.com • page 88: © Ints Vikmanis | Dreamstime.com • page 92: © Milo Cress • pages 96–97: © Lunamarina | Dreamstime.com • page 100: © Monkey Business Images | Dreamstime.com • page 103: © Dmitry Ersler | Dreamstime.com • page 104: © Toby Zerna / Newspix / Rex USA • page 105: © Maigi | Dreamstime.com • pages 106–107: © Jeroen Kins | Dreamstime.com • page 109: © Ron Chapple | Dreamstime.com • pages 110–111: © istockphoto.com/ShaneKato • page 113: © Kmiragaya | Dreamstime.com • page 113: © istockphoto.com/RBFried • page 114: © Rmarmion | Dreamstime.com • pages 114–115: © Milous Chab | Dreamstime.com

10 9 8 7 6 5 4 3 2 1
Printed in the United States of America
B10951012

Free Spirit Publishing Inc.
Minneapolis, MN
(612) 338-2068
help4kids@freespirit.com
www.freespirit.com

Printed on recycled paper

including 10% post-consumer waste

FSC
www.fsc.org
MIX
Paper from responsible sources
FSC® C008955

Free Spirit offers competitive pricing.
Contact edsales@freespirit.com for pricing information on multiple quantity purchases.

Dedication

From Cathryn: To my daughters Ariel and Devora, who keep me inspired to work toward caring for our planet for future generations.

From Philippe: To my niece Clementine, who inspires me every day and reminds me of the power of hope and optimism and our responsibility to pass on a better world to the next generation.

Acknowledgments

Our appreciation goes to all who gave their time, stories, and words to fill these pages. With special gratitude to:

- EarthEcho International—Mia DeMezza, Kyra Kristof, Ricky Hutchinson, and their Board of Directors—for their collaboration and joy brought to this endeavor.

- Free Spirit Publishing, especially Judy Galbraith for being such an environmental enthusiast and Meg Bratsch for her excellent editing.

- Paula Keener at NOAA's Office of Ocean Exploration for her thorough scientific review.

- Karla Blecke, Kaori and Doug Brown, Nate Ivy, Michelle Kamenov, Jill Peterson, and Megan Sparks.

- Alison Barrett at the Monterey Bay Aquarium, who introduced us to Makana.

- Marieta Francis, executive director at Algalita Marine Research Foundation, for the information on plastics and the five gyres.

- Zahra Dowlatabadi and Jim Biehold for their valuable assistance in creating the *Make a Splash!* book video.

- From Cathryn: Always my deepest appreciation is to my husband Barry, who gives me continual encouragement and love.

Contents

Introduction 1

Chapter 1: Find Out Why Water Matters.................................14

Chapter 2: Dive In to Discover the Deeper Story of Water.................50

Chapter 3: Get Going and Take Action for Water!......................84

Chapter 4: Think Back and Reflect on Your Actions.......................106

Chapter 5: Show It and Share Your Story with Others....................110

What's Next? 116

Words to Know..118

Watery Websites and Bubbly Books 119

Splashy Sources 121

Index..122

About the Authors 124

Introduction

Philippe's Story

Philippe Cousteau is the grandson of famous ocean explorer Captain Jacques-Yves Cousteau. Philippe has loved the ocean ever since he was a kid. Here he tells his story as someone who speaks up for water:

Young Philippe with his grandfather Jacques

As a young boy, I always looked forward to going to the beach. I especially remember one family trip to Hawaii. My sister Alexandra and I loved the tidal pools—the pools of water left behind after the ocean's tide washed up over the rocks. We'd run down to the beach every day to explore them. Together we leaned over the edge of the rocks and stayed as quiet and still as we could. What we saw was a whole community, a tiny world full of life. We watched many different creatures— pinching crabs, colorful sea stars, darting fish, and countless more.

1

A few years later, when I was 11 years old, I got to go on my first scuba dive in the ocean. The day was beautiful . . . and also sad. We were with a diver who had been exploring the area for many years. He described how the coral reefs used to be healthy and colorful. Now the coral was dying. Fish were disappearing. While we swam alongside him through the underwater world, we could see what he meant.

As I grew up, I kept exploring the ocean. I learned how important water is for all forms of life. I learned this, in part, from my grandfather, Jacques-Yves Cousteau. He was a world famous underwater explorer and filmmaker. The best word to describe him was *curious*. He was curious about the world. He especially loved investigating and exploring the Mediterranean Sea from his home country of France.

I got to go on my first scuba dive in the ocean. The day was beautiful . . . and also sad.

My grandfather wanted to spend all the time he could underwater. To do this, he partnered with an engineer named Emile Gagnan. Together they invented an air tank people could wear when they dove into the ocean. The tank allowed divers to breathe underwater for periods of time longer than ever before. We call this **scuba** gear. My grandfather also helped invent special underwater cameras and many other helpful tools.

Through my grandfather's TV programs and films, many people saw the world inside the ocean for the first time. They learned to care more about the environment. I learned this, too. My grandfather and my father, Philippe Cousteau Sr., taught me by example that we must always care for our planet—especially its water.

Now I share that message. These days I meet kids all around the world who care about Earth and its waters. They care about the oceans, seas, streams, rivers, lakes, ponds, and swamps that are in their own backyards. They also care about waters that are far away. They want to protect animals that live in

Define It
Scuba stands for self-contained underwater breathing apparatus. Scuba gear allows people to breathe underwater and go on long dives.

the water. They want people to have clean, safe drinking water. They want to do something big to help. They *can*—and so can you.

Make a Splash! will help you get started. You will learn amazing facts. You'll gather important tools and tips. You'll read stories about kids just like you who are taking steps to save and protect waters everywhere.

You can inspire and lead other kids and adults, too. Have you ever bugged your mom or dad for something you wanted? Well, you can also bug your family, neighbors, teachers, and friends to do something good for the environment! And you can show them the way.

Yellowstone River

Today, one of my favorite places in the world to spend time is by the Yellowstone River in the western United States. This river is full of trout and other fish. Bears and caribou drink at the water's edge. When we work together, we can save special places like this one.

I hope you find *your* special water place, too. It may be a river, stream, pond, marsh, beach, tidal pool, or coral reef. I hope you do your best to protect this place forever. So start reading, and get ready to make a splash!

Philippe Cousteau

How to Use This Book

How you use this book is up to you. Maybe you'll dive in and read it from start to finish. Or maybe you'd rather jump into the book at different spots. You might find a certain subject that interests you, or see a picture or drawing that catches your eye. That's fine, too.

However you decide to read this book, here's a handy guide to use along the way. Keep your eyes open for these bits and pieces:

Dive Log

Do you already have a special water place like Philippe does? Maybe a pond, creek, marsh, lake, river, coastline, or beach that you really love. Why is it special to you? What are some ways you can protect and care for it? Start a "Dive Log"—a journal, either in a notebook or on a computer—and make a drawing of this place. Gather some photos, too, if you can. Keep this special water place in mind as you read this book.

Define It

If you see a word in **bold**, look for a Define It box close by. These boxes explain words that might be new to you.

WATER WISE

What do you already know about water? What will you find out? Spark your interest with these Water Wise questions at the start of chapters 1–3. There's so much to explore! As you read, you'll find answers to the questions. (The answers are also at the bottom of each page of questions.)

Fluid Fact

Love facts and figures? These are just for you! Fluid Fact boxes are filled with splashy statistics and drippy details about water.

EarthEcho Tip

EarthEcho International is an environmental education organization founded by Philippe Cousteau and his sister, Alexandra. These tips will give you some of their ideas for caring for Earth's water.

KIDS IN ACTION

Ready for inspiring stories about kids around the globe taking action to protect water? Look for Kids in Action sprinkled throughout the book. You'll find practical ideas and helpful suggestions to use in your home, school, or community.

Every Drop Counts

The ideas in Every Drop Counts boxes came from second graders at Round Rock Elementary School in Texas. Water supplies were low in their town, and students investigated how people can save water. They learned that we have a limited amount of water on Earth, so every drop counts. The students made Water Conservation Kits to hand out to people. Each kit included a list of ways we can all save water.

Soak It Up

At the end of each chapter, look for the Soak It Up section. This brief chapter review helps you think about what you have learned so far and gets you ready for what's coming next.

At the very end of the book, you'll find a handy glossary of terms and a list of books, websites, and other resources. They'll help you continue making a splash to help water.

What does it mean to *make a splash*? The saying, "She made a splash!" means that the person did something that got a lot of attention. When you take the steps and suggestions in this book, you'll "make a splash" of your own to help save and protect our planet's water.

What Is Service Learning?

In *Make a Splash!* you will learn a lot about water—from where it is to why it needs our help. You'll also learn about *service learning*. What is it? Here's a simple way to remember: **service + learning = service learning.**

Service means doing something to help other people, animals, or the earth.

Learning means finding out more about a subject, or developing a skill by practicing.

A boy explores animal life along an ocean coast

When you put these two things together, you get **service learning.** During service learning, you learn about a topic that interests you, and then you do something related to that topic to help others. Around the world, kids are doing service learning for water. They are learning about real water needs and concerns. They are coming up with helpful ideas, and they are putting those ideas into action.

Service learning is made up of five parts. The chapters in this book are divided into those five parts:

1. **Find Out** (also called *Investigate*)
2. **Dive In** (also called *Prepare*)
3. **Get Going!** (also called *Act*)
4. **Think Back . . .**
   (also called *Reflect*)
5. **Show It!**
   (also called *Demonstrate*)

You can think of each of these as part of a big adventure—an underwater dive!

Students inspect a shoreline in Hawaii

Getting Ready for Your Dive

Every diver needs supplies. These supplies will help you through the five parts of service learning. Here is what you will take with you on your dive:

Mask to Find Out: Masks help you keep your eyes open wide as you **investigate** water and why it matters. With your mask on, look at the water around you. Where is water? How is water part of your everyday life? How is it part of your community? Who and what needs water to survive? Where is water in trouble? Ask others what they know about water. Find out about water needs and how you can help.

Snorkel to *Dive In*: A snorkel helps you breathe underwater so you can put your head under the surface and see what's beneath. With your snorkel on, you can look closer at the source of all water: the oceans. What are the biggest problems for our oceans? What is causing these problems? How are all the waters around you (like lakes, rivers, and swamps) affected by the oceans? Use what you learn to prepare to help water. You might talk to experts about a problem you've spotted. Research water stories online, in newspapers, or in books. Discover what other kids are doing for water. Being prepared with knowledge helps you get to the next stage: Action.

Flippers to *Get Going*: When divers slip on a pair of flippers, they *really* start moving. With your good ideas and expert knowledge, you can **act** on your plan to save our waters. Involve friends and your class, family, and neighbors. They can help with planning and spreading the word about your action. How can you make real change? What can you do to inspire others to join? How can you make sure your actions succeed? This is an exciting part of your dive— it's time to kick forward and make a splash!

Dive Log to *Think Back*: Divers keep track of each dive in a dive log. This helps them think back and **reflect** on their adventure. Your own Dive Log is a place to write, draw, add photos, and collect news articles. It's where you will record your ideas, thoughts, and feelings about your adventure. In fact, you've already used it on page 4 to write about your special water place. You might keep your Dive Log in a notebook of recycled paper. You could make your own notebook out of scrap paper. Or maybe you'd rather use a computer or other device. Whatever your log looks like, it's time to get it out when you see this symbol.

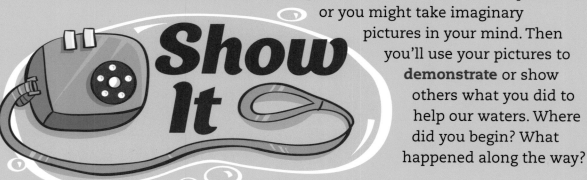

Underwater Camera to *Show It*: Finally, many divers take a camera with them on their dives so they can snap pictures. With your underwater camera, you will capture all that you see and do on your service learning adventure. You might use a real camera to take pictures, or you might take imaginary pictures in your mind. Then you'll use your pictures to **demonstrate** or show others what you did to help our waters. Where did you begin? What happened along the way?

What surprised you the most? Share what you know, speak up for water! Some kids make posters, put on plays, or create blogs. There are so many different ways to show what you did and inspire others to do something, too.

Grab your dive kit and let's go!

To help you understand the five parts of your dive, each part will begin with **The Story of Ogallala.** "The story of Oga-*what*?" Read on to find out.

Chapter 1:
FIND OUT
Why Water Matters

The Story of Ogallala: Part 1

Friona, Texas, United States

In the town of Friona, Texas, you won't find a big lake, river, or ocean. What you *will* find are playa [PLY-ah] lakes. Playa lakes only form when it rains, and rain doesn't happen in Friona very often. Playa lakes can look like small ponds or large puddles. The rainwater in them slowly trickles down into the underground water supply.

Friona's playa lakes trickle into the Ogallala (oh-ga-LA-la) Aquifer. This **aquifer** is one of the largest in the world. It is so large it stretches under eight states! Most of the water in it is pumped out to water crops that grow food for people and animals. Under the town of Friona, however, there is *less* water in the Ogallala than in any other place in the aquifer.

Playa lakes

Define It

An **aquifer** (AH-kwi-fer) is an underground layer of rock or soil that contains water.

How Did They Find Out?

Fifth-grade students set out to investigate why there is less water under Friona. They asked questions about Texas's playa lakes and about the Ogallala Aquifer. They asked: "What would happen if our water was gone from the playa lakes and the aquifer? How would our food grow?"

To find out, the students read local newspapers and websites. They learned that a **drought** in Texas was making big problems for the entire state. Then they interviewed farmers and water specialists to learn more about the problem and the need to save water. Next, they did a survey—they asked their parents and neighbors questions about how the changes had affected the area. They asked people what they knew about the playa lakes and the aquifer.

Finally, the students decided to observe the problem for themselves. They visited the playa lakes and looked at the plants and animals that live around them. They saw how little water there was in the lakes and how dry the surrounding area had become.

All of this investigation helped the students realize something. Most Friona residents did not know what a playa lake was. They also didn't understand the importance of the Ogallala Aquifer . . .

(This story continues on page 51.)

Define It

A **drought** is severe lack of rain in an area for a long time. A drought can result in low water supplies. It also makes it very difficult to grow crops for food.

Where Is Water?

Sure, you see water every day, wherever you live. Do you ever stop to *really* look at it and think about it? It's time to start seeing water clearly. So put on your mask to find out more.

In one form or another, water is all around you. That's true even if you live far away from an ocean, river, or lake. Clouds in the sky are made of tiny drops of water. And just like in Friona, water is also in the ground under your feet. Groundwater is a huge source of Earth's water. In fact, there is about 100 times as much water in the ground as there is in *all* the lakes and rivers in the world!

WATER WISE

1. Where is there more water: in all the world's lakes and rivers combined or underground?
2. Do wetlands—also called bogs and marshes—make our water dirtier or cleaner?
3. What uses the most water inside our homes?
4. What business uses the most water around the world?
5. What are two reasons why plants drink water?

Answers: 1. Underground. 2. Cleaner. 3. Toilets. 4. Agriculture. 5. Nutrients and cooling.

So a lot of water is in the ground. However, most of the planet's water is in the ocean. Take a look at this photo of Earth. It shows our planet from outer space. What color do you see the most?

Blue. All of that blue is water. Maybe this isn't Planet Earth after all. Maybe we really live on Planet Water! Earth's oceans are really one big ocean divided into five basins: the Atlantic, Pacific, Indian, Southern, and Arctic ocean basins. An ocean basin is like a giant bowl of water.

These five ocean basins are connected, just like *all* water on Earth is connected. How is it connected? Through a complex puzzle of lakes, rivers, streams, and swamps. And also through something called the *water cycle*. Here's how it works: First, water **evaporates** from the ground and from bodies of water. Some of this water becomes clouds in the sky. Some of the water stays in the air. Does the air outside ever feel wet to you, or humid? That means a lot of water is in it.

Next, water falls back to Earth as rain, snow, sleet, or hail. Then, water soaks in the ground or flows into our rivers, lakes, marshes, and oceans. Finally, water evaporates again into the air and the clouds. The cycle continues, on and on and on and on . . .

Define It
When water **evaporates** it turns from a liquid into an invisible gas. The water seems to simply disappear, because we can't see gases floating through the air. But it's still there!

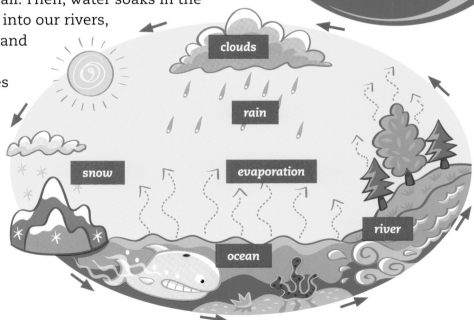

clouds

rain

snow

evaporation

river

ocean

The Water Cycle

Same Water, Different Time

This might be news to you: Earth's water supply has never changed. *Ever*. We've had the same water all through time. The water on our planet today is the same water that dinosaurs drank over 200 million years ago. It just keeps going around and around through the water cycle.

Over 200 million years ago

150 million years ago

The Water in Your Backyard

So water is in the air above you and in the ground below you. Where can you *see* the water around you? Can you spot it rippling in a creek or sparkling in a pond? Maybe after a rainstorm you see water running down the gutters in your street.

Or maybe you don't see much water where you live. It might be hidden. Still, water is there somewhere. Water even exists in the desert! This water may be far below the surface. Or it may come in a very rare rainfall, as it does in Friona. Either way, it's there. Without water, cactuses, lizards, and other desert dwellers couldn't survive.

Water is always on the move, all around you.

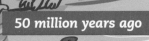

50 million years ago

Now

Watersheds are what connect this moving water. Our whole planet is one big watershed that eventually drains into the ocean. Within this giant watershed, thousands of smaller watersheds connect together.

Watersheds are busy places. They are homes to plants, trees, large animals, and tiny insects. They come in many sizes and shapes, and they often stretch across cities, counties, states, provinces, and countries.

Let's look at the main parts of the watershed puzzle: lakes, rivers, wetlands, estuaries, and ocean coasts. We'll see how they fit together and why each is important.

Define It

A **watershed** is an area of land where all the water that is in or under it flows into the same place.

Dive Log

Go on a water treasure hunt in your neighborhood! Hop on your bike, take a walk with a friend, or ask an adult to come along as you explore. Find a creek. Spot a swamp. Or follow a trickle of water in your street. Does the water you've found meet up with other water? Where? In your Dive Log, record the results of your water treasure hunt. Draw a map, paint a picture, or write a story about the way water fits together where you live.

Lakes

A lake is a body of water surrounded by land. Most lakes hold fresh (not salty) water. At some times of the year, a lake can be a dry basin waiting for water from rivers and rain to fill it. Lakes can form from landslides and glaciers (huge slow-moving chunks of ice). River bends and volcanic craters that fill with rain can become lakes, too. People can also make lakes by building dams in rivers.

Lakes are home to a variety of plants and animals—including many kinds of freshwater fish, turtles, and frogs that only live in lakes. Lakes also provide drinking water to many people around the world. And if you live near lakes, you know they're *sensational* for swimming!

Rivers, Streams, and Creeks

Rivers, streams, and creeks flow across (and sometimes under) Earth's surface. They carry fresh water. They often begin on hills or mountains. A large, rushing river may start as a small stream or creek. As a tiny creek gathers water from rain or an underground spring, it can grow into a river.

Rivers can be used to make electricity by moving large machines with the rushing water. They're also used to water crops and transport supplies. They help keep factories going, crops growing, and people moving. Rivers, streams, and creeks also provide water for plants and animals along the shore.

Wetlands

Have you seen a swamp, bog, or marsh? These important areas are called wetlands. Just like their name says, they contain wet land. They are places that store water temporarily as it slowly moves from one place to another. They can be freshwater or saltwater, depending on how close they are to the ocean coast.

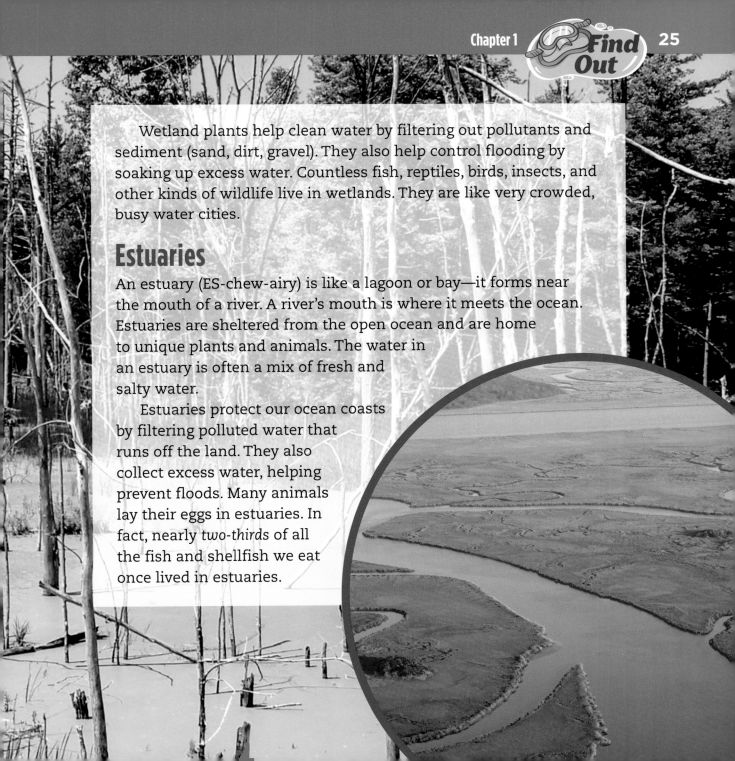

Wetland plants help clean water by filtering out pollutants and sediment (sand, dirt, gravel). They also help control flooding by soaking up excess water. Countless fish, reptiles, birds, insects, and other kinds of wildlife live in wetlands. They are like very crowded, busy water cities.

Estuaries

An estuary (ES-chew-airy) is like a lagoon or bay—it forms near the mouth of a river. A river's mouth is where it meets the ocean. Estuaries are sheltered from the open ocean and are home to unique plants and animals. The water in an estuary is often a mix of fresh and salty water.

Estuaries protect our ocean coasts by filtering polluted water that runs off the land. They also collect excess water, helping prevent floods. Many animals lay their eggs in estuaries. In fact, nearly two-thirds of all the fish and shellfish we eat once lived in estuaries.

Ocean Coasts

The coasts of the world's oceans are on the edges of huge continents and tiny islands. Some coasts are rocky. Some are sandy beaches. Sometimes a coast is a high cliff plunging into the water below. Other times, a coast is made up of gently rolling sand dunes or a grassy field.

Ocean coasts are popular for many residents and visitors. People build sand castles and sail, surf, and splash in the waves. Birds and other animals live in coastal grasses and shrubs. Sandy beaches are nesting grounds for sea turtles and some small fish.

Your Piece of the Watershed

All the pieces of a watershed fit together like a puzzle.

What pieces are near you?

KIDS IN ACTION
EL CERRITO, CALIFORNIA, UNITED STATES

Knowing Our Watershed

Kids at Prospect Sierra Schools in northern California live near the Baxter Creek watershed. Kindergartners and second graders explored the area. They listened to frogs croaking at sunset. They watched mallard ducks eating quietly. They saw shimmery green dragonflies with huge eyes. They studied rock carvings made by people who lived by the creek a long time ago. Learning all these things inspired the kids to keep the creek healthy. They picked up trash along the creek's banks to help keep the water clean. **They wanted other people to care about their watershed, too.** So they wrote a book describing its plants and creatures. It was called *From the Tops of the Trees to the Bottom of the Pond: A Field Guide to Canyon Trail Park.*

Watersheds link all our bodies of water together. So keeping every part of the watershed clean matters. The students in El Cerrito (see opposite page) did their part to protect their piece of the watershed and to teach others about it.

From Stream to Sink

Now you know more about where water is in the world. Here's a question that's closer to home: When water comes out of your kitchen or bathroom faucet, where does that water come from?

The answer depends on where you live. The water might come from a river or stream that flows near you, or from a lake or reservoir (a human-made lake) somewhere outside your city or town. The water might come from a well in the ground. Water wells go far down into the earth and pull up groundwater. Or, your water might be from a combination of places.

From a stream, lake, or reservoir, big pipes take the water to a water treatment plant. There, the water gets cleaned and filtered. This removes any dangerous germs or chemicals that might have come along with the water. Other pipes carry the clean water out of the plant. These pipes go under streets, sidewalks, playgrounds, and parks. They split into smaller pipes that go to businesses, schools, and homes like yours. Then even *smaller* pipes carry the water through your home to your sink. Finally, after you use it, the water goes back down the drain and starts its journey all over again.

Every Drop Counts

When you do dishes by hand, fill up the sink with soapy water instead of letting the water run. You'll use much less water that way.

Drinking Water's Journey

stream

water treatment plant

pipes

pipe carrying dirty water
back to treatment plant

house

sink

pipe carrying clean water
from treatment plant to sink

Dive Log

Where does your drinking water come from? Find out if your water supply company has a website you can visit. Search the Internet for the name of your town, city, or region, and the words "water supply." You might even be able to visit your water treatment plant. Record in your Dive Log what you learn and see. You could draw a map or a picture, or write a story about a water drop's journey from its source to your sink.

EarthEcho Tip

Watch out for leaky faucets! A single drippy faucet can waste up to 150 gallons (or 560 liters) of water a day. That's enough to fill your whole bathtub *three times*. If you find a leak at home or school, ask an adult to help you fix it as soon as possible. While it's leaking, try to save the water in a bowl or bucket. You can use it later to water plants, wash dishes, or meet other water needs.

People Need Water

Water matters to every person, everywhere on Earth, every single day. Why? Because people are made mostly of water, and they need water to stay alive.

You're Made of Water!

brain: 75% water

lungs: 90% water

full body: 70% water

You are all wet, all the time—even when you're not swimming or bathing. How is that possible? Because you're wet on the *inside*. The tiny building blocks of your body are called cells. These cells are made mostly of water. Take a look at these numbers:

- Your brain is nearly **75 percent** water.

- Your lungs are **90 percent** water.

- Your bones are **20 percent** water.

- Overall, your body is **70 percent water!**

We need to drink water often to keep our bodies healthy and strong. Going even a couple of days without drinking water can make a person very sick. If people go much more than five days without water, they will die.

Water also makes our lives better. After you go for a bike ride, play a sport, jog, or dance, a cool glass of water refreshes you. And on a hot day, jumping in a lake or running through a sprinkler can feel like the best thing ever.

But guess what? **Our water supply on Earth is limited.** Here are some more water numbers to think about:

- **97 percent** of the world's water is in the ocean. The problem is, this water is too salty for people and most animals to drink.

- **2 percent** of Earth's water is frozen in glaciers and ice. So it's not drinkable either.

- Only **1 percent** of the water in the world is unfrozen fresh water. That's how much we have for *all* living things to drink—people, animals, and plants.

We all share this 1 percent of drinking water. People around the world don't all use the same amount of water, though. **People in the United States use the most: an average of 150 gallons (or 560 liters) of water per person every day.** What about the rest of the world? This chart shows how much water people use in different countries.

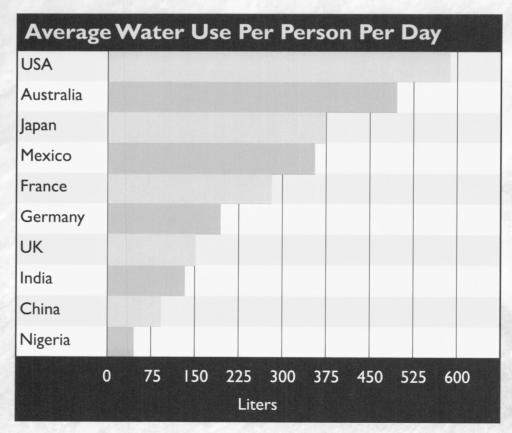

Average Water Use Per Person Per Day

Country	Liters
USA	~560
Australia	~490
Japan	~375
Mexico	~360
France	~290
Germany	~220
UK	~150
India	~135
China	~85
Nigeria	~30

Note: 1 liter equals slightly more than 1 quart.

Fluid Fact

Can we make *new* fresh water to drink? In many parts of the world, people change salty seawater into fresh water by taking out the salt. However, remember that all water on Earth eventually flows back into the ocean. Taking out too much salt from our water now could later harm plants and animals in our oceans that need salty water to survive. In other places, waste from toilet water is removed. The clean water is put back into fresh water systems. Unfortunately, this takes lots of energy. We need *better* solutions that don't hurt our ocean life and that use less energy.

Tap into Water

When you are thirsty, what do you do? You fill a glass of water from the faucet, maybe. Or you take a drink from a water fountain. Not everyone can do this. In many parts of the world, clean water is not always available. Adults and children often become sick and die of thirst. Or they die of disease caused by dirty water. Why?

Our population is growing. About 7 billion people now live on Earth. We might have 9 billion by 2050.

Every Drop Counts

If you pour yourself a glass of water and you can't finish it, put it in the fridge for later.

Meanwhile, our water supply is *not* growing. Here are some more facts:

- **Less rain is falling around the world.** Droughts are becoming more common and more serious. One example is the severe drought that happened in the midwestern United States during the summer of 2012. It was the largest drought in nearly 60 years, ruining many crops and reducing traffic on the Mississippi River.

- **Earth's climate is changing.** As the planet gets warmer, more water evaporates into the air. That leaves less water to drink.

- **Pollution is making water dirty.** Toxic liquids flow from cars, trucks, boats, factories, and farms into bodies of water. This pollution leads to unsafe drinking water. It can also kill fish and other animals.

- **People are using too much groundwater.** This means our store of underground water (called the *water table*) is too low for what is needed.

- **Long-term water shortages are now common**, especially in North Africa and Western and South Asia.

With all of these problems, how can all the people on Earth expect clean drinking water every day? Around the world, people (including kids!) are trying to think of ways to save and protect clean water.

KIDS IN ACTION
IZMIR, TURKEY

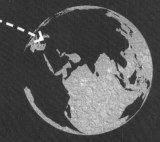

Water Drops with a Message

The country of Turkey is in a dry part of the world. Saving water there matters a lot. In the city of Izmir, a group of young students decided to help spread this message. **They dressed up as little blue water drops.** Then, in the city's main square, they put on a play about water drops. Older children chased the little water drops, showing that people are thirsty and need water. After the show, the little water drops went up to people in the audience. They handed out stickers with information about saving water. They asked people to put these stickers in their kitchens and bathrooms to remind them to use less water. They also made a video of the play to help teach other kids about saving water. These little drops made a big splash! Watch their video on youtube.com, search: Water Drops: Message to Humanity.

Turkish kids dressed as water drops

Water Use by the Numbers

We all use water to drink. We also use water for many other purposes. Take a look at how much water we use for a few daily actions:

Tip: Imagine a big gallon jug of water to get an idea of these amounts.

When you ...	you use about ...
Flush a toilet	6 gallons per flush
Wash your hands	2 gallons
Brush your teeth (with water running)	10 gallons
Take a shower	Up to 10 gallons per minute
Fill a bathtub	35 gallons
Run a washing machine	Up to 55 gallons

Note: 1 gallon equals about 3.8 liters.

This doesn't even include the water we use to cook food, wash dishes, water lawns, transport goods, and create electricity.

KIDS IN ACTION
NOVA SCOTIA, CANADA

Rocks in the Pot

Ecole Saint Catherine's School Roots & Shoots team in Halifax, Nova Scotia, invited a representative from Clean Nova Scotia to their school to talk about saving water. Afterward, students decided to install water reservoirs in the school's 45 toilets. Students collected 500mL plastic bottles from recycling bins. They filled them with water and pebbles. Then, they put two bottles in every toilet tank, reducing each flush from 13 liters to 12. While that may not seem like a lot, it adds up—*fast*.

EarthEcho Tip

What if all of us spent about six seconds fewer in the shower every day? This little change would make a gigantic difference. In the United States alone this would save *85 billion gallons (or 322 billion liters)* of water per year. That's about 130,000 Olympic-sized swimming pools! Can you shorten your shower a little bit each day? What about using a little less water in the bathtub?

Water for Food

Can you guess what people use the most water for? More than drinking, washing, and cooking combined? Farming. *Two-thirds* of all the water we use goes into watering crops that grow vegetables and grains for you to eat. It's used to water the crops that feed the animals you eat, too, if you eat meat.

What can *you* do to help? You can eat less meat, because so much water is required to produce it. You can also save water by eating locally grown food. Most food travels about 1,200 miles before landing on your plate! Salmon from Alaska. Tomatoes from Mexico. Apple juice from China. It takes a lot of energy (and water) to move all this food from place to place. Trucks, trains, planes, and boats that carry food and other goods create pollution that makes our air and water dirty.

Fluid Fact

400 gallons (or 1,500 liters) of water are needed to produce one pound of wheat.

2,000 gallons (or 7,500 liters) of water are needed to produce one pound of beef.

Water for Power

The second biggest use of water is for industry. Manufacturing plants use electricity. Making electricity takes water—*a lot of it.* Water helps run the machines that produce electricity. Water also helps cool down these machines so they don't get too hot. Turn the page to read what kids in Colorado did to save water by saving electricity.

Dive Log

List the ways you use water daily at home and at school. Be sure to think about the food you eat and the energy you use. Ask others how they use water. Then, brainstorm ways to use *less* water every day. Share your list!

KIDS IN ACTION
CARBONDALE, COLORADO, UNITED STATES

Save Energy = Save Water

Kids at Crystal River Elementary School had a mission to save water by saving energy in their school. Here are some of their actions:

- On handprints cut out of recycled paper, they wrote tips for saving energy. Then they posted these "handy" reminders all over school.

- They left lights off in classrooms and the cafeteria on sunny days.

- They checked all doors and windows to see if cold air was getting in during the winter. Buildings with air leaks need more heat. That means extra energy. The same thing happens in summer. Air conditioners have to work extra hard when cool air slips out.

- They asked kitchen workers to turn off and unplug big appliances that were not needed over weekends and holidays.

- That school year, the school saved about $18,000 in energy bills. That means a lot of water was saved, too!

Animals Need Water

Just like people, animals need water to live. Do you have a pet? If so, you know it's important to give your cat, dog, hamster, or bird fresh, clean water to drink every day.

Many animals also need clean water to live *in*. Think about a fish in a river. They breathe by taking in water through their gills. If trash or poisonous chemicals are dumped into the river, the fish get sick. Animals that depend on that same water to drink may get sick, too.

Or imagine a beaver family that builds a dam on a pond. If people build a factory near the pond, the water could get very dirty and make the beavers sick. Or people might build a parking lot on top of the pond. Then, beavers and other pond animals lose their homes and have trouble finding food and new places to live.

If you care about animals, then you also need to care about water.

EarthEcho Tip

Do you like to go camping? Make sure that you take care of the water around your campground. Be careful not to pour dishwashing soap into a lake or spit toothpaste into a stream. You may be hurting animals that live in or near that water. Whenever you're in nature, remember to watch out for our waters.

KIDS IN ACTION
CHUBUT PROVINCE, ARGENTINA

Trees and Water Go Together

Argentina's Los Alerces National Park is full of lakes and wetlands. When a fire destroyed much of the park's forests and grasses, its animals were in danger. The water was in danger, too. The trees and plants prevented chemicals in the soil from running into the water. Also, their leaves soaked up gas in the air that can be bad for the water. Kids at a nearby elementary school, Delia Medici de Chayep, wanted to help. They listened carefully as park rangers taught them how to grow helpful plants. Together, they planted 1,500 new trees, bushes, and other plants that would help rebuild the park and protect its water.

Plants Need Water, Too

Have you ever grown a plant? What does it need? Water!

What happens if you forget to water your mom's favorite geranium on the windowsill? First, the plant's leaves droop. Then, they turn brown or yellow. Next, the plant dries out and its leaves and flowers start to break off. Only water can save that plant. Plants "drink" water through their roots, stems, and leaves. Water carries food from the soil into the plant. It also helps plants cool down in the hot sun.

Farmers depend on water to care for the plants in their crops. If there is a drought, the crops will die unless farmers find water. Sometimes they dig deep wells to find groundwater. People in India have even dug their own ponds (sometimes by hand) to collect rainwater for their crops.

When you care for water, you are also caring for plants.

Every Drop Counts

When you give pets a bath, try to bathe them outside on an area of grass that needs water. Remember to fill up a bucket with water to use instead of letting the hose run.

KIDS IN ACTION
SINGAPORE

Marvelous Mangroves

Have you ever seen mangroves? These beautiful trees grow in clusters along our ocean coasts in many parts of the world. Mangroves help protect water and are home to numerous animals. In the small island country of Singapore, entire mangrove forests have been cut down to make room for hotels and houses. A group called Cicada Tree Eco-Place decided to do something. They invite visitors to take a boat ride to a tiny island called Pulau Ubin to view healthy mangrove forests. There, they show adults and kids how special these trees are. **They teach visitors how they can help protect mangroves and join with others to plant new trees.** Kids in the United Arab Emirates, Malaysia, and Indonesia are helping, too! Visit mangroveactionproject.org to see how you can get involved.

Earth Needs Water

All of Earth's animals, plants, and water are connected. Our whole planet is one big, living community. Earth is made up of 70 percent water, so caring for our water is a *very* big deal. We need to make sure that clean water is available for people, plants, and animals everywhere. We must protect our home—after all, it's the only one we've got!

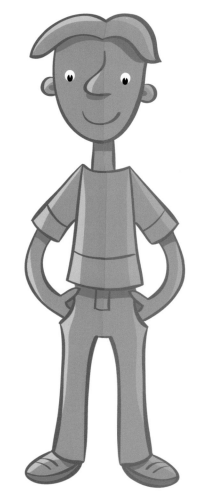

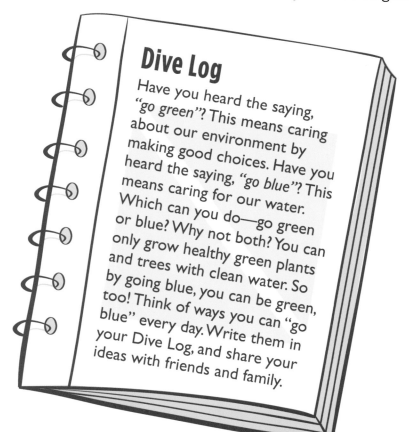

Dive Log

Have you heard the saying, "go green"? This means caring about our environment by making good choices. Have you heard the saying, "go blue"? This means caring for our water. Which can you do—go green or blue? Why not both? You can only grow healthy green plants and trees with clean water. So by going blue, you can be green, too! Think of ways you can "go blue" every day. Write them in your Dive Log, and share your ideas with friends and family.

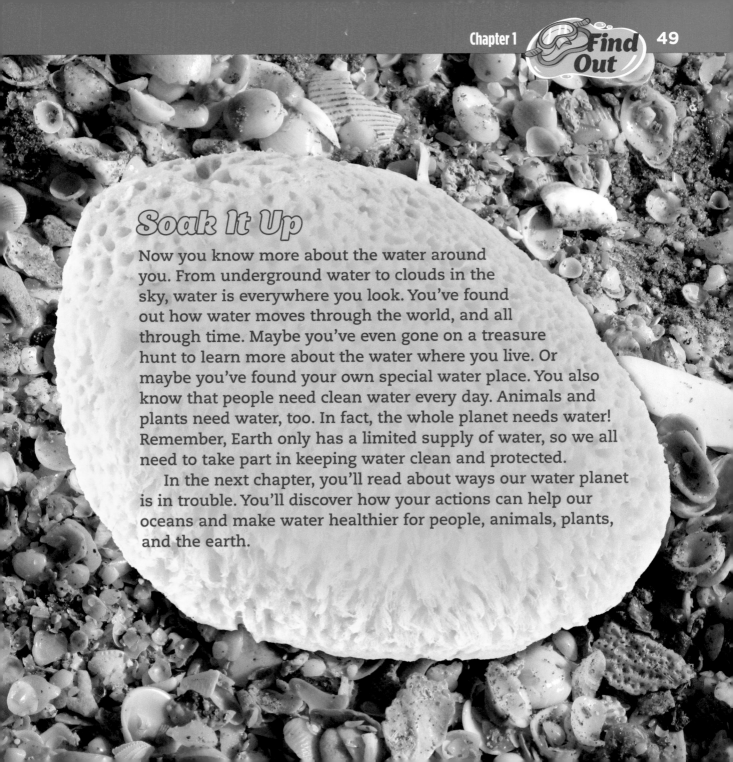

Soak It Up

Now you know more about the water around you. From underground water to clouds in the sky, water is everywhere you look. You've found out how water moves through the world, and all through time. Maybe you've even gone on a treasure hunt to learn more about the water where you live. Or maybe you've found your own special water place. You also know that people need clean water every day. Animals and plants need water, too. In fact, the whole planet needs water! Remember, Earth only has a limited supply of water, so we all need to take part in keeping water clean and protected.

In the next chapter, you'll read about ways our water planet is in trouble. You'll discover how your actions can help our oceans and make water healthier for people, animals, plants, and the earth.

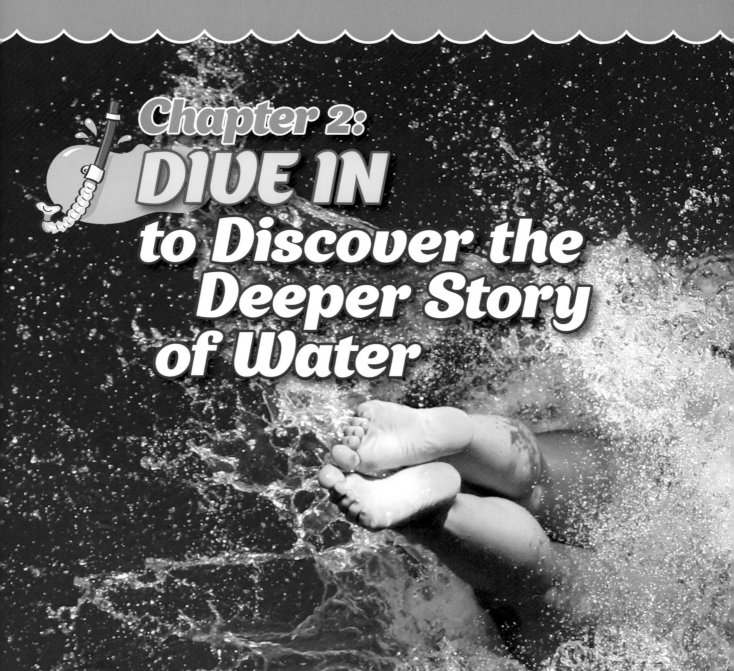

Chapter 2:
DIVE IN
to Discover the Deeper Story of Water

The Story of Ogallala: Part 2
Friona, Texas, United States

How Did They Dive In?

The Friona fifth graders decided to help their waters by educating people about playa lakes and the Ogallala Aquifer. To prepare to do this, the students read all they could about playa lakes and aquifers. They learned new vocabulary words. They looked at many photographs of these underground waterways and saw how they're connected. They discovered how weather and climate affects playa lakes and aquifers, and how they, in turn, affect other waterways—including the ocean. Fortunately, the students had good help in understanding these topics! Friona high school students led lessons for the fifth graders, and together, everyone became smarter about water.

Armed with all they learned, the students decided it was time to act . . .

(This story continues on page 85.)

The Big Blue Ocean

All the water on our planet matters. By caring for water close to you, you're caring for water everywhere—even in the ocean. That's because all of Earth's water is connected, from the water in your bathtub to the water in Friona's playa lakes. And all of it flows toward one source: the ocean.

In Chapter 1, you looked through your mask to start really *seeing* the water all around you. You found out about water needs in your community and around the world. **Are you ready to swim farther—all the way to the middle of the ocean?** Do you want to discover the many ways the ocean matters to your life? Slide on your snorkel . . . and dive in!

> "We all live upstream from one another. No matter where you live, your actions affect our world's oceans and waterways."
>
> —Philippe Cousteau

Protecting our oceans means protecting the air we breathe. About 50 to 70 percent of the oxygen on Earth comes from the ocean. That's more oxygen than we get from all of the world's rainforests combined! How does the ocean produce oxygen? Millions of tiny plants called *phytoplankton* (fy-dough-PLANK-ton) live in the ocean. Like other plants, they turn sunlight into food. As they do this, they make oxygen. People, animals, and plants need this oxygen to live.

WATER WISE

As you read the chapter, watch for the answers to these water questions.

1. What is the most common greenhouse gas that people make?

2. Where is North America's only living barrier coral reef?

3. How many pounds (or kilograms) of plastic trash enter the world's oceans every hour?

4. What is upcycling?

5. What was the first country in the world to ban plastic bags?

Answers: 1. Carbon dioxide. 2. Right off the Florida Keys. 3. 2.4 million pounds (or 1.1 million kilograms). 4. Taking something old or worn out and making it into something different and better than before. 5. Bangladesh.

Here are some other good reasons to care about our ocean:

- The ocean is home to some of the world's smallest living creatures—called bacteria.

- The ocean is also home to the world's largest animal: the blue whale. Blue whales can grow to be about 100 feet (over 30 meters) long. That's longer than two big school buses put together!

- Nearly half the world's people live on or near ocean coasts.

- More than 1 billion people depend on ocean fish and other seafood as a main source of nutrition every day.

Oil + Water = A Poisonous Mess

On April 20, 2010, the Deepwater Horizon oil rig exploded in the Gulf of Mexico. Eleven people died. Millions of barrels of oil spilled into the Gulf. The oil reached the shores of Texas, Louisiana, Mississippi, Alabama, and Florida. The government, environmental groups, businesses, and concerned people all took action to help clean up this oily mess. Philippe Cousteau was one of those people. Here's his story:

66 Like people all over the world, I watched the story of the Gulf oil spill on television. I was very worried about the damage to animals, people, and the environment. I decided to go to the Gulf to see what happened. People who work there took me on boat rides to see the damage along the coast. I flew in an airplane to get a bird's-eye view of the disaster.

Clams and a sea turtle covered in oil

I saw the massive spill. I saw dolphins, birds, and sea turtles suffering and dying. Beaches, wetlands, and coastal areas were covered in black slime.

Next I went diving into the oil spill. I had to wear special protective gear all over my body. I looked like an astronaut. My gear kept me safe from the dangerous chemicals in the water.

Usually when I dive into the ocean, the water is a beautiful blue-green. Normally I see many animals swim by. This time, however, I had to swim through a big dark cloud of muck and goo floating on the surface. I didn't see *any* living animals—just dead fish and weeds covered in oil. I felt very sad.

I saw dolphins, birds, and sea turtles suffering and dying. Beaches, wetlands, and coastal areas were covered in black slime.

I also visited people who lived along the Gulf's coast. Many were losing their jobs. Lots of local businesses depended on fishing and tourism. The spill stopped these businesses. Still, there were people willing to work hard and help out. I met many kids who were upset and worried. They wanted to change what was happening to their communities and their planet.

Is the danger over today? No. Some of the area has been cleaned up, but the oil and chemicals still damage animals and plants. And people are still taking action. Every time I go back to the Gulf, I meet more people who work daily to clean the water and help protect the coast. Many of these helpers are children, just like you. The Gulf of Mexico will need our help for years to come. What would you like to do? "

Sea bird covered in oil

Dive Log

Do you remember the Gulf oil spill in 2010? If not, ask some older kids or adults about their memories of the oil spill. How did they feel when it happened? What did they do to help? What are some ways they (and you) can still help today?

KIDS IN ACTION
OAKLAND, CALIFORNIA, UNITED STATES

The Clean Team

Students at Park Day School live more than 2,000 miles (or 3,200 kilometers) away from the Gulf of Mexico oil spill. Even so, they still pitched in to help with the recovery. At school, fourth graders learned that some cleaning products contain chemicals that are bad for water. They wanted people to think twice about the products they use. They also wanted to help with the Gulf cleanup. **So they found out how to make household cleaning products that are safe for the environment.** They made samples of these products and gave them creative names like Zoink, Mr. Moo, and Adios Germose. The kids advertised their products at a local farmers market and showed them to parents, too. They sold their samples and sent the money to Mobile Baykeeper in Alabama. This environmental group has hosted Philippe Cousteau on many of his trips to the Gulf Coast.

Our Oceans Are in Danger

As the world saw in the Gulf of Mexico, oil spills are a serious problem for our oceans. After a spill, a layer of thick oil spreads over the water, killing most small animals. Even if bigger animals can swim away, they often get sick and later die. Chemicals in the oil poison plants, too. It can take decades or more for a beach to recover from an oil spill.

Unfortunately, oil spills aren't the only threat to our waters. Other big problems include climate change, trash, pollution, and fishing.

A Changing Climate

One of the biggest problems facing our oceans is climate change. Climate change means that our planet's temperatures are getting warmer. The waters are getting warmer, too. That doesn't mean that every place on Earth is getting hotter each day. Instead, it means that temperatures are rising on average over time.

Some climate change is natural. Earth's climate has cycles and patterns. Temperatures rise and fall. However, most scientists agree that human actions have made these changes bigger and faster. Human actions can also help slow down these changes. For more information, let's hear from two young weather reporters from Sedalia, Missouri, named Reagan and McKenna . . .

The Oceans Need Your Help!

Reagan: "Today we're going to talk about climate change and how it affects our oceans."

McKenna: "Then we'll tell you what *you* can do to help."

Reagan: "Greenhouse gases are a big cause of climate change. These are gases that build up in the air and make our planet warmer. Carbon dioxide is a common greenhouse gas. When we burn oil and coal to run cars, factories, electrical plants, and farms, we produce *a lot* of carbon dioxide. Some of it stays in the air and some of it goes into the water."

McKenna: "Our oceans absorb up to half of this carbon dioxide. It causes the water to have more acid in it. Water that has a lot of acid is bad for many ocean animals, because it makes it hard for them to build their shells. Without strong shells, they die."

Reagan: "Other ocean animals and plants need the water to be a certain temperature. As greenhouse gases make the water warmer, these animals and plants have to move from their homes to find cooler water."

McKenna: "All these changes with animals and plants mess up the ocean **food chain.** If this keeps happening, people who depend on ocean fish for food will not have enough to eat."

Reagan: "What can we do? One big step is to reduce how much carbon dioxide we make. There are lots of ways to do that. Cars and electrical plants produce a lot of carbon dioxide. Instead of riding in cars, you can walk, bike, or take a bus. You can turn off lights and unplug electronics when you are not using them. Remember: If an appliance is plugged in, it is using up electricity—*even* if it's turned off.

McKenna: "Factories that make new products also add carbon dioxide to our air and water. You can help by recycling and reusing as many things as you can. Then, encourage other people to do the same. Remember: *Every little bit helps.*"

Both together: "That's today's weather report. Over and out!"

Define It

A **food chain** is a system where living things (plants and animals) feed on other living things. *Example:* algae is food for a minnow → the minnow is food for a fish → the fish is dinner for you. Each link in the chain depends on every other link. Food chains all connect together to create Earth's food web.

KIDS IN ACTION
WESTERLY, RHODE ISLAND, UNITED STATES

TGIF: *Turn Grease into Fuel*

Fifth graders in Westerly learned that oil from ships and cars isn't the only threat to our waters. Cooking oil is a problem, too. When people pour grease down a sink drain, it pollutes the water system. It is also a huge waste of oil! Students set out to find a solution. **They discovered that used cooking oil can be turned into a fuel called *biodiesel*.** Biodiesel can be used to heat the homes of families in need. Plus, it gives off less carbon dioxide than other kinds of heat. So the students asked local restaurants to donate their grease to be recycled into biodiesel. They set up recycling containers and now have over 108 restaurants participating. Next, students met with their state legislators and convinced them to pass the Used Cooking Oil Recycling Act. It says that, as of January 1, 2012, all businesses in Rhode Island *must* recycle their used cooking oil.

Westerly students making biodiesel

"I'm Melting!"

Here's a cold, hard fact: Climate change is also causing Earth's glaciers to melt. Glacier National Park in the United States and Canada could be *without* glaciers by the year 2030. The entire Arctic Ocean may be ice-free by 2040. What will this huge amount of melting ice do to our waters? To our climate? To plants and animals? To us?

One problem is that it will create floods. For example, as ice melts in mountain regions, lakes overflow. The water that spills over can flood whole villages. Another problem is that when glaciers melt, fresh water flows into the salty ocean. This changes the way warm and cold currents move through the ocean. These currents affect the temperature of our air on land. They can cause severe heat waves and cold snaps.

Extreme temperatures also cause changes in our weather. Do you have hurricanes or tornadoes where you live? Because of climate change, these storms are happening more and getting stronger and more dangerous.

Fluid Fact

As the planet warms, plants and animals everywhere are moving to cooler climates. How far are they moving? About one mile per year.

Coral Reefs in Trouble

All animals, no matter where they are, need water to live. And animals that live right *in* the water are the first to suffer when water is in trouble. Of all the places to live in the water, coral reefs are special. They are some of the oceans' most prized habitats. It's easy to see why. Healthy coral reefs are full of bright colors, amazing shapes, and millions of fish and other creatures. They are home to 25 percent of all ocean life!

Coral may look like a rock at first glance. Look more closely, and you'll see that it is actually a collection of animals. Coral reefs are made up of groups of tiny animals called coral polyps. Each coral polyp uses limestone to make a little shell to live in. Together, the coral polyps create a whole building of tiny, stony apartments. This apartment building has homes for plants, fish, ocean sponges, sea stars, anemones, snails, sea snakes, sea turtles, and countless other animals.

Dive Log

What do you see in the photos of coral reefs on the next page? What don't you see in each photo? How do these photos make you feel? Imagine a coral reef as an apartment building. In your Dive Log, write a story about or draw pictures of the building and the animals that live in it.

The problem is, coral reefs are in serious trouble. They are very sensitive. When ocean water changes, reefs can suffer and die. Water temperature is important for healthy reefs. So is the amount of acid in the water. That means that greenhouse gases and climate change are a major threat to coral reefs and all the plants and animals that live in them. **Studies predict that *half* of all coral could be gone from our oceans by the year 2050. What can we do?**

Healthy coral reef

Dying coral reef

KIDS IN ACTION
BIG PINE KEY, FLORIDA, UNITED STATES

Caring for Coral

Kids at Big Pine Academy really care about the ocean. After all, they see ocean waves right out their window. They live in the Florida Keys, a chain of about 1,700 islands that was formed from coral reefs. North America's only living coral barrier reef is located right off the Florida Keys. The students read about and explored their area. They went snorkeling in the water and looked at the coral. They were worried about the coral reef dying. **So they made a plan to help repair the reefs.** With help from high school students, the kids put together modules—pieces of cement with pipes on top. These modules became places for new coral to grow. The older students went scuba diving and set up the modules underwater. All of the kids made displays to teach others to care for coral, too.

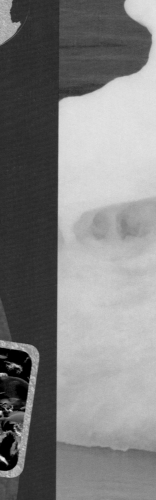

Animals at Risk

The many threats to our oceans are bad news for animals. As you've learned, coral reefs and the creatures that live in and around them are in trouble. Water problems cause trouble for many other animals, too.

For whales and dolphins, a growing concern is underwater noise. Humans make a lot of noise in the ocean. Boats roar their engines. Oil drills rumble. Military ships use loud underground sounds to find submarines. Human-made noise in the water can confuse dolphins and whales and cause them to struggle to find food and mates. Scientists think that too much loud noise can cause extreme pain and even brain damage in these creatures. To try to escape from painful noises, some whales and dolphins swim out of the water onto beaches. There, they die.

Melting ice is a problem for polar bears. They spend most of their lives on ice. That's where they hunt for food and raise their families. **As climate change causes glaciers and polar ice to melt, the polar bears' homes disappear and they can't always find enough to eat.** And they sometimes have to swim a long way between pieces of ice. Some bears starve or drown.

Polar bear on shrinking ice

Melting ice is also troubling for sea turtles. Sea turtles lay their eggs on sandy beaches. As ice melts, sea levels rise and beaches shrink. When beaches get smaller, sea turtles have a hard time finding places to lay their eggs. Also, as people build along ocean coasts, they often destroy sea turtles' homes.

Baby sea turtle traveling from the nest to the sea

Too Much Fishing

Another growing concern for our oceans is fishing. People have been fishing for their food for centuries. **Now, with more than 7 billion people on the planet, there's more fishing than ever.** Fish is the most important source of food for over a billion people on Earth.

Years ago, people used to eat only the fish and seafood that came from where they lived. Now, tuna caught in Japan is flown all the way to Germany. Shrimp from Thailand ends up in Texas. This means more fish are being caught. In some places, too much fishing—called *overfishing*—hurts the ocean and the animals that live there. Some types of fish have almost disappeared. This is bad news for the ocean food chain.

Overfishing can also badly damage coral reefs. Many large fishing boats drag huge nets and heavy traps along the ocean floor. They destroy reefs and sweep up many creatures in their path. Then the fishing crews throw back the dead and hurt animals they don't want. This is a horrible waste! Read about what kids in California and Japan are doing to save the kings of all fish . . .

Turtle and coral tangled in fishing nets

KIDS IN ACTION
IRVINE, CALIFORNIA, UNITED STATES;
AND YOKOHAMA, JAPAN

Sticking Up for Sharks

Kids at Eastshore Elementary School in Irvine, California, learned all about sharks. They discovered that each year over 40 million sharks are caught and "finned" (their fins are cut off) to make shark fin soup. Then, they are tossed back in the water to die. As a result, sharks are becoming endangered. Sharks are an important part of the ocean food web, and if they disappear it would cause big problems for *all* sea life. Eastshore students decided to take action to protect sharks. They made presentations to show other kids that sharks are important and not evil. (Sharks *very rarely* attack people.) They designed "I Love Sharks" T-shirts that were sold by local stores. Students donated the money to organizations that help protect sharks. They wrote articles about sharks and shark finning for newsletters and magazines. They started a Stop Shark Finning Pledge Campaign online and collected over 1,000 pledges. **Then, they met with their state senators and the governor's staff to get support for a bill banning the sale of shark fins in California.** In October 2011, it became a law! Students made sure to tell others about all their actions on the website they created: ilovesharks.org.

Kids in Japan also want to protect sharks. Fourth and fifth graders at the Yokohama International School heard about shark finning. They learned that many people in Japan buy shark fins, especially in Yokohama's Chinatown neighborhood. The students took action and gave presentations to teach other kids about sharks. They made posters and put them up around school. They talked with restaurant owners in Chinatown about the issue. **They started a Save the Sharks Pledge Campaign online through the Roots & Shoots program.** They also started a blog to keep everyone up-to-date on their activities and shark finning news. You can visit it here: blogs.yis.ac.jp/rootsandshoots.

> "Continued shark finning will cause the shark population to disappear, destroying our beautiful ocean."
>
> —Sachi, age 10, Yokohama, Japan

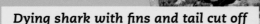
Dying shark with fins and tail cut off

Terrible Trash

As if shark finning, overfishing, and climate change were not enough . . . our oceans also must battle trash. *Tons* of it. Trash pollutes the oceans and all of Earth's water. It puts many animals in danger, too. Read on to find out more about this problem from an expert named Makana.

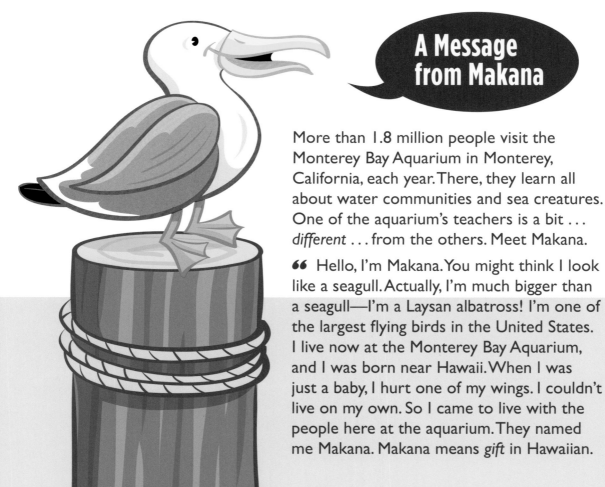

A Message from Makana

More than 1.8 million people visit the Monterey Bay Aquarium in Monterey, California, each year. There, they learn all about water communities and sea creatures. One of the aquarium's teachers is a bit . . . *different* . . . from the others. Meet Makana.

66 Hello, I'm Makana. You might think I look like a seagull. Actually, I'm much bigger than a seagull—I'm a Laysan albatross! I'm one of the largest flying birds in the United States. I live now at the Monterey Bay Aquarium, and I was born near Hawaii. When I was just a baby, I hurt one of my wings. I couldn't live on my own. So I came to live with the people here at the aquarium. They named me Makana. Makana means *gift* in Hawaiian.

My favorite part of each day happens at 1:30 p.m. That's when I get to meet visitors, like you. An aquarium guide explains where I am from and what I eat. The visitors admire my huge white wings. Then they learn about a big problem for birds like me: *Trash*.

As a human, you probably see trash in many places. Snack bags, bottles, cans, and wrappers litter your sidewalks and streets. Do you ever wonder where it all goes? I can tell you. Much of it flows into street drains when it rains. From there it travels through pipes that empty into lakes, rivers, and our oceans.

How does this affect me? In the wild, albatrosses like me fly over the ocean searching for food. Sadly, we also find all kinds of trash.

About half of this trash is plastic. Everything from toothbrushes to rain boots to car parts. Over time, plastic breaks into very tiny pieces that look like food to us. We eat this plastic by mistake. It fills our stomachs, but it's not food. We end up starving to death.

Animals can also get cut or tangled up in bigger pieces of trash. If we can't breathe or we bleed a lot, we'll die.

Every day here at the aquarium, kids discover how the trash in our oceans hurts animals like me. These kids want to help make the world safer for all of us. You can help, too! "

Makana

Dive Log
Write a letter to Makana. Tell her what *you* will do to protect seabirds and other wildlife.

Aim for Zero

The less waste we make, the more water we save. Can you make zero waste? You can start by making a zero-waste meal like kids did in Pasadena, California, at the Polytechnic School. Try to eat all of the food, reuse all the containers, and recycle any leftovers in a compost heap (see page 80 for more on composting).

Here are some more zero-waste tips from the Polytechnic students:

- Make colorful posters about zero waste and hang them in your school's lunch area.

- Set up a display showing zero-waste food and beverage containers.

- Use lunch boxes or cloth bags instead of paper or plastic.

- Use reusable silverware, containers, and thermoses.

- Pack washable cloth napkins instead of paper.

- Avoid plastic baggies, plastic straws, and aluminum foil.

Polytechnic kids eating zero-waste lunches

Fluid Fact

People make 300 billion pounds of plastic each year, and right now, we only recycle about 5 percent of that amount. An estimated 2.4 million pounds (or 1.1 million kilograms) of plastic trash enters the world's oceans every hour. That weighs about as much as 170 elephants! Sunlight slowly breaks down plastic into tiny pieces. However, plastic never disappears completely. It will still be here centuries from now.

The (Not-So) Great Pacific Garbage Patch

So where does all this trash go when it enters the ocean? Much of it goes into a gigantic floating garbage dump. It's called the Great Pacific Garbage Patch and it's located between California and Hawaii. **It's about twice as big as the state of Texas. Experts think it doubles in size every 10 years.** What's in it? Computer parts, car tires, shoes, toys, bottles, and much more. Most of it is plastic.

There are huge garbage patches in other parts of the ocean, too. And the trash isn't limited to these patches—it's spread all over the ocean. Unless we change our ways and stop making so much trash, this "plastic soup" will grow until there is no clean ocean left.

Every Drop Counts

Try to avoid plastic toys—especially ones that *also* waste a lot of water, like giant squirt guns.

Bottled Up

A big portion of these floating garbage dumps is plastic water bottles. They make up most of the world's plastic trash. Many of these bottles aren't recycled.

What does this mean for us and our waters? Here are some bottled water facts:

About 40 percent of bottled water starts out as tap water.

The process of making a plastic water bottle uses three times the amount of water than the bottle holds.

Once the water is in the bottle, dangerous chemicals from the plastic can get into the water.

9 out of 10 plastic water bottles end up as trash. That's 30 million bottles in the garbage—enough to fill 42 *Titanic* ships every day.

Reusable water bottles are a smart solution!

KIDS IN ACTION
SEDALIA, MISSOURI, UNITED STATES

The Anti-Bottle Project

Fourth graders at Heber Hunt Elementary School learned about water from each other. Yelena used to live in Russia, where her home did not have water. Instead, her family had to carry water inside from a street faucet or collect rain water in tubs. Carlos was from a small village in Mexico where people got their water from a well. They put their used water into a pond where they raised fish to eat. Cristian came from El Salvador where water supplies were often low. Government trucks came by with drinking water for villagers. Everyone only got a small amount.

After hearing these stories, the class talked about the importance of clean drinking water. At the same school, first graders learned how plastic water bottles can hurt our planet. Together, the Heber Hunt kids made a plan to help water. **They joined the Anti-Bottle Project and sold colorful reusable water bottles at school.** Together they made posters and gave a lively presentation about protecting and saving water. **They also designed bookmarks to give out with the bottles.** The bookmark listed ways to use less water. These tips were in three languages: English, Russian, and Spanish. The students sold all of their "anti-bottles" in just one hour! This meant a lot fewer plastic bottles would be going in the trash in their school. Visit randomkid .org/content/130/117 to find out more and to join the movement. Also, check out Vapur Anti-Bottles at vapur.us.

The Trail of Trash

Even if we stop using plastic water bottles, we can't stop making trash completely. We can learn to throw it away properly so that it doesn't end up in our water. So where exactly is "away"?

Some trash that we put in our garbage cans goes to landfills. **Landfills are huge mountains of garbage. They often sit on land for years and rot.** Rotting trash can produce a gas called *methane*. Methane is a greenhouse gas, like carbon dioxide, and can contribute to climate change. Other trash from our garbage cans is burned at factories. Unfortunately, burning trash can also create chemicals that pollute our air.

The good news is that we can recycle some of our trash. This trash goes to a recycling plant where it is made into something else. For example, an aluminum soda can is usually turned into a new can. We also help our earth by composting some of our trash. Composting is a process that turns certain kinds of garbage into healthy soil that helps plants grow.

Landfill near a beach

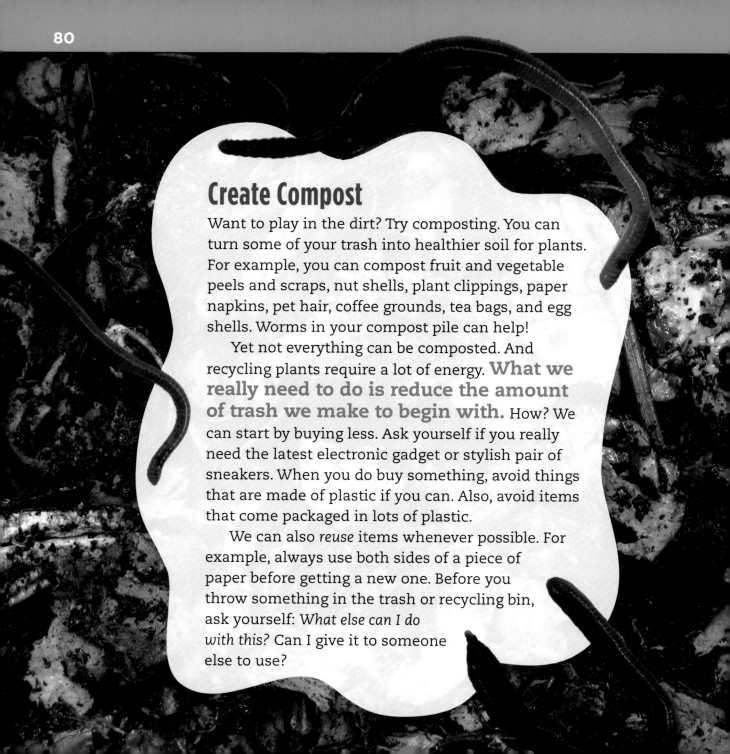

Create Compost

Want to play in the dirt? Try composting. You can turn some of your trash into healthier soil for plants. For example, you can compost fruit and vegetable peels and scraps, nut shells, plant clippings, paper napkins, pet hair, coffee grounds, tea bags, and egg shells. Worms in your compost pile can help!

Yet not everything can be composted. And recycling plants require a lot of energy. **What we really need to do is reduce the amount of trash we make to begin with.** How? We can start by buying less. Ask yourself if you really need the latest electronic gadget or stylish pair of sneakers. When you do buy something, avoid things that are made of plastic if you can. Also, avoid items that come packaged in lots of plastic.

We can also *reuse* items whenever possible. For example, always use both sides of a piece of paper before getting a new one. Before you throw something in the trash or recycling bin, ask yourself: *What else can I do with this?* Can I give it to someone else to use?

EarthEcho Tip

Have you heard the word *upcycle*? It's a little different than recycle. To upcycle means to take something old or worn out and make it into something different and better than before. That way you save the energy it takes to make a brand new product. For example, you can turn an old sweatshirt into a laptop or tablet carrying case. You can cover a tin can with used paper, tie it with a ribbon and make a vase. Get creative! Be an upcycler! Visit terracycle.com to learn more and join an international campaign.

Every Drop Counts

Recycle your water, too! If you have water left from an activity, use it for something else.

Old bottle used as a vase

Bracelet made from soda can tabs

KIDS IN ACTION
BUCHAREST, ROMANIA

Better Bags

At the American International School of Bucharest, kids learned that plastic bags are a big part of the swirling mess in our planet's waters. They clog rivers and wash up on beaches. **So they joined Jane Goodall's Reusable Bag Campaign to encourage people to use reusable bags.** They made posters for the school and designed and sold colorful cloth bags. Then, they used the money to make more reusable bags to sell. Good-bye, plastic!

Students in Bucharest

Fluid Fact

In 2002, Bangladesh was the first country in the world to ban the use and production of plastic shopping bags. On January 1, 2011, Italy became the first country in Europe to ban plastic bags. Several cities across the United States, England, Canada, Mexico, Australia, India, and other countries have similar bans.

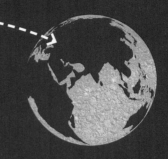

Soak It Up

In this chapter, you've read about the source of all of Earth's water: the oceans. And you've learned that our oceans have big problems. Oil spills, climate change, melting ice, plastic trash, and overfishing threaten the oceans' health. Coral reefs are in danger. So are many, many animals and plants. Fortunately, there are ways to tackle these problems. You've already read lots of tips for helping the Earth's waters. Ready for more? The next chapter is just what you need to take big action. Be prepared for buckets full of ideas for planning and carrying out your plan. Get ready for real, rippling results!

Dive Log

What have you learned so far about the ocean that really surprises you? Did anything make you sad? Mad? Worried? Inspired to take action? What do you want to learn more about? How can you share what you know with someone else?

Chapter 3:
GET GOING
and Take Action
for Water!

The Story of Ogallala: Part 3
Friona, Texas, United States

How Did They Get Going?

The fifth graders and high school students in Friona were ready for action! They joined forces to form a team called the "Playa Posse." Together, they planned and led the town's first ever Playa Lake Festival. For three days in the fall, students gathered their community members to celebrate and learn about playa lakes and the mighty Ogallala Aquifer. They brought in water experts to teach people about water cycles, animal and plant habitats, droughts, and water conservation. They performed original plays and told stories. They made models to show how the playa lakes form and their importance. They painted beautiful murals to help everyone appreciate the area's unique ecosystem. They also designed games, so all ages could join in the fun.

Throughout the year, the Playa Posse provided community education about the playa lakes and the aquifer. They wrote articles for the local newspaper and made videos to show others. The fifth graders led a parent night where they taught parents about these valuable water resources and how much Friona's families depend on them.

(This story continues on page 107.)

Getting Ready for Action

What's on your mind? Which water issue grabs you? Droughts? Trash in the ocean? Pollution in a pond near your home? Sea turtles in danger? Or maybe a Kids in Action story made you think *"I can do that!"* You've put on your mask to find out about water needs around the world. You slid on your snorkel to dive in to learn all about the ocean. Now it's time to slip on those flippers and *really* get going to make a big difference for water!

WATER WISE

As you read the chapter, watch for the answers to these water questions.

1. What is the most common form of litter in the world?
2. What did a boy named Milo do to reduce the number of plastic straws in our waters?
3. How do you conduct a "water audit"?
4. How much water can you save by turning off the tap while you brush your teeth?
5. Why might penguins need to wear sweaters after an oil spill?

As the Kids in Action stories in this book show, there are different ways to take action for water. Here are four kinds of action: direct action, indirect action, advocacy, and research. You can pick one kind of action, or combine them. **Which kind of action will you choose?**

Answers: 1. Cigarette butts. 2. He asked restaurant owners to offer people straws instead of automatically giving them one. 3. Check for any ways water use can be reduced and make a list. 4. 25 gallons (95 liters). 5. To prevent them from eating oil when they clean their feathers.

1. Direct Action: Be a Role Model

Your actions can help water immediately. They can also help you be a role model for others. By showing you care about water, you will inspire others to care, too. By taking direct action, you might join a litter cleanup like the yearly Ocean Conservancy International Coastal Cleanup (oceanconservancy.org). Then, you might do like the *Plant Your Butts* kids (see page 89) and come up with a way to make less trash to clean up.

Fluid Fact

If you looked at litter around the globe, you would see more cigarette butts than anything else. People litter about 4.5 trillion cigarette butts each year. Many of them end up in the water.

KIDS IN ACTION
KAILUA, HAWAII, UNITED STATES

Plant Your Butts

Kids at Huakailani School in Hawaii pick up trash three times a year as part of a community program. One time, they noticed a lot of cigarette butts. Within several blocks, they counted almost 2,000 butts. Yuck! They asked people why they tossed their butts on the ground. The most common answer was, "These butts are so small, they can't matter." Wrong! Wind and rain carry cigarette butts into the water supply and eventually the ocean. The butts contain poisons that can kill sea animals and plants. **The students decided to provide planters where people could "plant" their butts instead of tossing them on the ground.** They put quarry sand inside (*not* beach sand, because it's harmful to remove sand from a beach). They decorated each one with paint and wrote "Plant Your Butts Here." Then they placed them outside shops and restaurants. During the next cleanup, the kids only found 700 cigarette butts! Watch their video on youtube.com, search: Plant Your Butts Here.

Student at Huakailani School

KIDS IN ACTION
LOS ANGELES, CALIFORNIA

Trash No More

Second graders at the John Thomas Dye School visited the nearby Ballona Wetlands. They learned about how pollution from cities hurts wetlands. After their visit, the kids wanted to donate money to help care for the Ballona Wetlands. They decided to hold a *Trash-a-Thon*. For one week, every day during recess, kids collected trash around school. **They asked people to give 1 to 10 cents for every piece of trash collected.** They picked up more than 1,330 pieces of trash, which equaled a lot of money!

The students sent the money to a group that helps protect the Ballona Wetlands. At school, they posted reminders to keep trash off the ground. With good ideas, planning, and fun, they helped their watershed.

John Thomas Dye kids picking up trash

2. Indirect Action: Be a Teacher and Helper

Remember the kids who came up with a list of ways to make *Every Drop Count* (see page 6)? They provided information so others can protect water every day. When action is indirect, you may not immediately see the results of the good work you do. However you are still helping people and our planet. How about writing a book—*The ABCs of Being Water Smart*? Or raising dollars for a pro-water cause, like the Clean Team (see page 58) and the kids in the story on the opposite page (page 90).

Every Drop Counts

Don't flush your toilet more than you need to. Don't use it as a trashcan just to get rid of bugs and garbage.

EarthEcho Tip

After you collect trash with a group of friends or as part of a cleanup, look at it! If you see many items from the same restaurant or shop, plan to make them your partner to inform customers about responsible trash disposal.

3. Advocacy: Be a Message Maker

What one watery issue or story do you care about the very most? Is a local stream polluted? Do you see water being wasted? Are there too many plastic water bottles everywhere? Telling others about this issue can be your action. This is called advocacy. Think about how you can share your important message. Design posters and pamphlets. Put on a play like the kids in Turkey (page 37). Make an action-packed video with friends. Be creative and think big! Get your message on radio, on television, or online. Send out a press release to the media (see page 104). A message that grows and reaches a lot of people becomes a campaign. A campaign can spread your message to other towns and cities— even to other countries! That's what happened in the next story.

Be Straw Free campaign poster

KIDS IN ACTION
BURLINGTON, VERMONT, UNITED STATES

Be Straw Free

Plastic drinking straws may seem like no big deal. But people around the world use *millions* of straws every single day and tons of them end up in the ocean. Shouldn't someone do something about this? Somebody did! Milo Cress started the Be Straw Free campaign. **He asked people who run restaurants to offer people straws rather than always putting them in drinks.** Soon, restaurant owners who joined Milo's campaign reported that their customers were using up to *80 percent fewer* straws! Milo also helped create bestrawfree.org. He reached out to people who make, sell, and use straws. Schools and businesses in the United States, Canada, and Malaysia signed up to help. Milo met with the mayor of his hometown. He agreed to help Milo make Burlington the first straw-free city in the United States. Milo hopes people everywhere will try to be straw free. And he encourages other kids to join him in taking action.

"You and I can create the future for our planet." —Milo Cress

Milo with his dog

KIDS IN ACTION
ST. PAUL, MINNESOTA, UNITED STATES

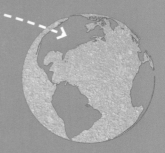

Loving Our Lakes

Kids at Farmsworth School live near lots of lakes. The fourth graders learned about these lakes and had lots of questions. How did the Dakota Indians use Minnesota's lakes before European settlers arrived? Why do lakes need to be clean? How does dirty water hurt animals and people? How have our lakes changed over the years? **The kids did research: they gathered facts to answer these questions.** They visited lakes near them. They met experts who work to protect lakes. They even pitched in and helped with that work. And then these students spread the word. They made a video and a handout telling others about the problems lakes face. At a community water festival, they showed other people how they could help find solutions.

Every Drop Counts

When you wash your hands, turn off the water while you rub the soap in. Also, turn off the water while you are brushing your teeth. You will save about 25 gallons (95 liters) of water per month!

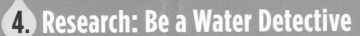

4. Research: Be a Water Detective

How can *research* be action? By researching information others can use to help save and protect water, you are acting as a successful water detective. Start at your school by doing a water audit. How? With permission, check for any ways water use can be reduced. Make a list of any leaks you find or times water is running that could be turned off. Take photos or draw pictures of what you see.

Dive Log

You've discovered what others have done . . . now it's time to plan your **own** action. Ask yourself: What issues matter the most to me? What can I do well? What activities sound like fun to me? List your answers in a "Me-List" in your Dive Log. Use your unique skills and interests to help water!

Show your evidence to decision-makers. Watch change happen! Or learn as much as you can about issues facing a local body of water. Then, make a list of questions that need answers and get others involved to help find solutions.

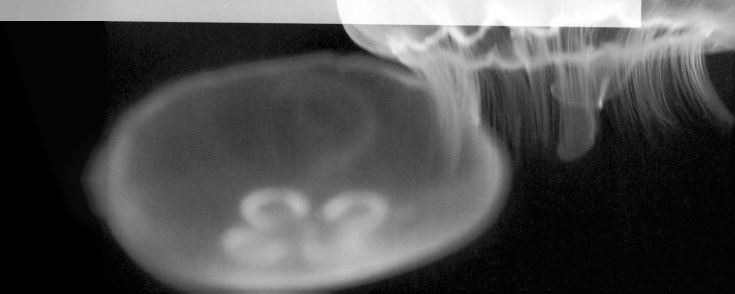

Build Your Water Squad!

Have you decided on a plan to help water? Then you're ready to gather a team to help you carry it out. Just like many drops of water make an ocean, many people can help bring your ideas to life. Who can help?

Adults want to be helpful. So give them jobs to do! Talk to parents, teachers, youth leaders, coaches, and other grown-ups about your idea. Explain what you want to do for water and why. Can they help you find out what other people in your community are doing for your water cause? Can they help you get the supplies you need to carry out your plan?

Kids your age probably want to help. Let them know. Ask them to join. Talk to kids at school, in your clubs, at your community center, and other places where you spend time. As your plan develops, your water action team can put up posters or make school-wide announcements to get more and more kids involved.

Older kids may help, too. Maybe you have a big brother or sister who wants to lend a hand. Do you know other older kids who have done service learning for water or another cause? Ask what they did. They may have good ideas and good advice. They might like your idea and want to pitch in.

By building a water squad, you can make your action plan grow from good to great!

Be Political

Even though you are too young to vote, you do have a voice. Our waters and the animals and plants living in them can't speak for themselves. *You* can be their voice.

- Remind your parents and other adults who *can* vote to think about water while they decide who to vote for.

- Identify the people in your local, state or provincial, and national governments. Search on the Internet or at a library, or talk to a teacher or other adult. Then, find out what water-related issues these people care about. What actions have they taken for water?

- With your class or group, invite elected officials to join your activities and be part of your cause. Write brief letters to tell them what you are doing for the environment. Ask them to join you at a cleanup or other event.

- Ask an adult to help you find out when your representatives are speaking near you.

Go to an event. Prepare a water-related question or two to ask during or afterward. Make a "Water Saving Tips" brochure to hand to him or her.

🔹 Visit local or state or provincial government offices. Get to know your officials and let them get to know you. Share your ideas. Teach these adults to be water smart.

Make a Plan

Once you've decided what you will do for water, let people know you mean business. Put your ideas into writing. This will be your *plan for action*. You can share it with others who can help, like teachers or parents or group leaders. It can help you raise donations of money or supplies.

Be sure to make your plan fun and attractive. That shows others that you have creative ideas and solutions. Add art, photos, or poems. Share your ideas the way *you* want to. Being a kid means you can do it your way! The next page shows a simple example of a plan for action.

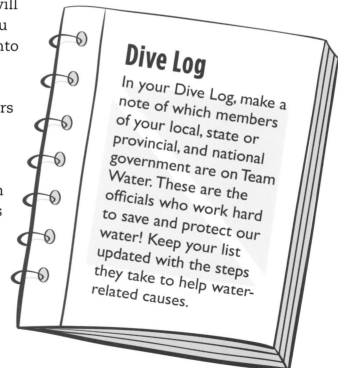

Dive Log

In your Dive Log, make a note of which members of your local, state or provincial, and national government are on Team Water. These are the officials who work hard to save and protect our water! Keep your list updated with the steps they take to help water-related causes.

Our Plan for Action

Students and Adult Leaders: Kendall, Brooklyn, and Seth, with Mrs. Clark and Mrs. Allen

Our School or Group: Students from Friona Elementary and Friona High Schools

Our Big Idea: Create the Playa Posse, a group of students who protect our playa lakes.

Our Problem: We have droughts. This threatens our water supply. For our everyday use and for agriculture, we have to save water all year long.

Our Solution: Educate the community about the importance of playa lakes, the Ogallala Aquifer, and saving water at all times—not just during droughts. We will have community displays all year long. We will hold a three-day Playa Water Festival for the community. With fun games, plays, experts, and useful ideas, all of Friona will be water wise.

Our Partners: Our local newspaper, local water district workers, and local farmers

Our Aim: Make water conservation important to all of Friona's residents through education and helpful tips.

Our Proof: Participation at the Playa Festival and testimonials from community members

Supplies We'll Need: Camera, computer, poster paper, art supplies

Our Timeline:

August–September: Investigate topic, prepare for festival

October: Take action by holding festival

November–February: Reflect on our actions, prepare demonstrations: create displays, videos, websites, articles, and plays

March: Show demonstrations of our actions, involving parents and community members

April–May: Evaluate the results of our actions, continue with our work at playa lakes: pick up trash and restore habitat areas with plantings of native species

Our Signatures:

Kendall   Seth   Mrs. Allen

Brooklyn   Mrs. Clark

Spread the Word

Once your plan for action is ready, tell others. Everyone loves a good story—and you have a great one. After all, water matters to everybody.

Who needs to know what you are doing? Who can help you? Do you need supplies? Transportation? Ideas? Could partners help with planting to stop erosion by a nearby creek? Do you need an audience for a water puppet show? Invite people to take part or to watch. Put a spotlight on your action.

The Ripple Effect

Sometimes you might only have a few moments to share your message. So make your time count. Try thinking about five little "ripples" of words to spread. Together, these ripples can add up to a big splash. You can speak your ripples, write them in a letter, or make a video. Maybe you'll tell your school's principal, a reporter, or even a governor. Here are descriptions of your five ripples:

Ripple 1: Share the main point of your big idea.
"Did you know that some household cleaners go down the drain and pollute our water?"

Ripple 2: Give more information.
"We did a study of five common products found under the sink at school and home. We learned that they all pollute."

Ripple 3: Tell what action you're taking.

"We started a new brand of homemade, safe household cleaners, like our all-purpose cleaner called Zoink."

Ripple 4: Explain how your action works.

"We sell products and use the money to restore places where water is in danger, like in the Gulf of Mexico."

Ripple 5: Invite the person you're talking with to get involved.

"We have our products right here. Would you like to take a look?"

Together, all your ripples can make a *big splash* of change!

Start the Presses

Your local media sources can be a big help in sharing news about your plans. Watch for news stories about water issues. Write down the reporter's name. This may be a good person to cover *your* story. How do you let all these people know about your plan for action? Create a press release! (See a sample on the next page.) The purpose is to attract people's attention and to let them know about your event. Send your press release to local TV and radio stations, websites, and newspapers. Share it with politicians and local groups that care about water. Post it on community blogs. Ask your water squad to help you follow up with phone calls and email reminders.

Remember: **Be brief. Be lively. Be YOU!**

Sample Press Release

FOR IMMEDIATE RELEASE:

Kids Knit for Penguins!
October 16—Albuquerque, New Mexico

catchy title

Did you hear? A ship near New Zealand just spilled 350 tons of oil into the water—covering many penguins! We must stop these birds from trying to clean the toxic oil off their feathers. So we are knitting sweaters to cover them, and we need you to help!

important information

who

If you want to knit or wish to learn how, come to Belle's Knit Shop where a team of kids and adults will get you started. Then we'll send the sweaters to penguins that need them!

what

Penguins in sweaters in New Zealand

when

Date: All Saturdays in November
Time: 10 a.m.–3 p.m.

where

Location: Belle's Knit Shop 1108 La Costa Way

For details, contact:
James Marc at
555-654-3210
or jm@bluemail.com

contact information

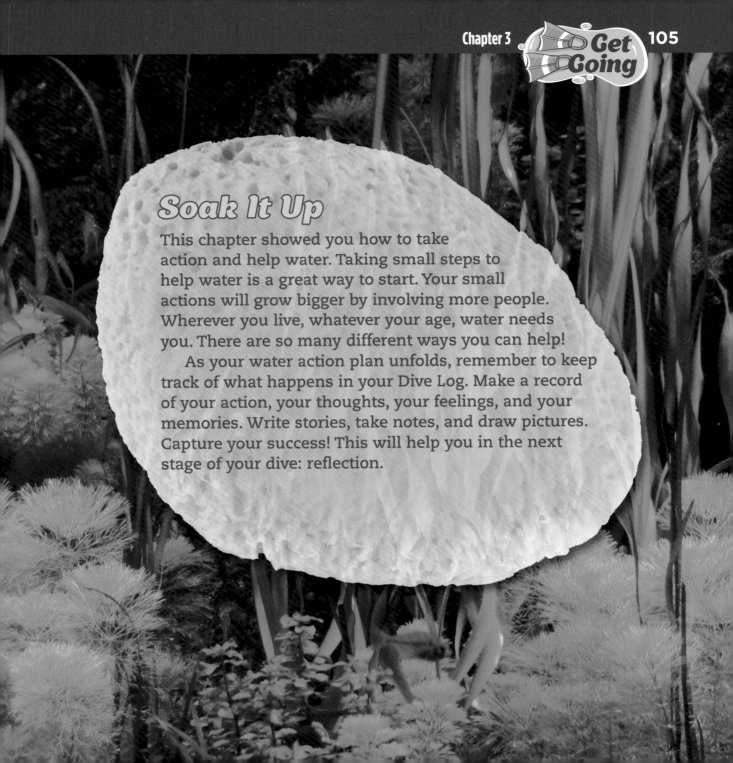

Soak It Up

This chapter showed you how to take action and help water. Taking small steps to help water is a great way to start. Your small actions will grow bigger by involving more people. Wherever you live, whatever your age, water needs you. There are so many different ways you can help!

As your water action plan unfolds, remember to keep track of what happens in your Dive Log. Make a record of your action, your thoughts, your feelings, and your memories. Write stories, take notes, and draw pictures. Capture your success! This will help you in the next stage of your dive: reflection.

Chapter 4:
THINK BACK and Reflect on Your Actions

The Story of Ogallala: Part 4

Friona, Texas, United States

How Did They Think Back?

"What did I learn about droughts, playa lakes, and aquifers?"
"Did my actions help others learn?"
"Did people like all our games and activities at the Playa Lake Festival?"
"Will people help save water to protect our community?"
"How did my skills and talents help the Playa Posse?"

All during their service learning experience, Friona's Playa Posse of students wrote, drew, talked about, and acted out their responses to these and other reflection questions. Pausing and thinking about their actions helped them learn what worked and what didn't. Sharing their thoughts and feelings with others helped them plan even better actions.

(This story continues on page 111.)

Remembering Your Dive

Throughout this book, the Dive Log boxes reminded you to pause and think back. Just like the Playa Posse did, you've kept a record of your actions, thoughts, and feelings. With everything you've learned, seen, and done, you must have a scintillating [SIN-tah-lating] story in your Dive Log!

Now is a perfect time to reflect on your entire water adventure. So browse through your Dive Log. Think back. Soak Up. Remember each stage of your dive.
Ask yourself some questions:

- What went especially well?
- What was my favorite part of taking action?
- What would I do differently next time?
- What have I changed about my daily habits to save and protect water?
- When did I feel most excited, scared, happy, sad, or hopeful during my journey so far?
- What did I learn about me and *my* talents?
- What will I do next?

As you think about your answers, you could talk about them with someone. You might also write or draw responses in your Dive Log.

Soak It Up

Have you ever floated on a raft, staring up at the clouds? Or sat quietly by a stream? Stopping to reflect on what's around us helps us pay attention. What a perfect time to take out your Dive Log! Sketch a frog on a lily pad, or write a poem about an ocean wave. Reflection can be a lot of fun, and it helps you get ready to share your story with others.

Chapter 5: SHOW IT and Share Your Story with Others

The Story of Ogallala: Part 5
Friona, Texas, United States

How Did They Show It?

Throughout everything they did, the Playa Posse of Friona showed their stuff. With all the photos and quotes they collected at the Playa Lakes Festival, students knew they would have stories to tell. They wrote these stories for Friona's newspaper and made photo displays to show in the community. In doing so, they informed many, many people of the importance of the playa lakes and the Ogallala Aquifer. They helped Friona's residents understand that we *all* have a part in saving our water. Fifth graders and high school students got to use their talents in planning, photographing, filming, writing, game designing, speaking, and blogging. The excitement became contagious as the Playa Posse grew into community superheroes!

Want to know how you can get involved and hold your own playa festival? Visit: playafestival.blogspot.com.

Once You Know It, Show It!

You've paused to think back on your action. Now it's time to take out the final piece in your dive kit—your underwater camera—and share your story. Maybe you saved water at home and also reduced water use at school. Maybe you fought pollution or picked up trash along a beach. Maybe you helped clean up a lake for the fish that live there. Or maybe you held a splashy community event, like the kids did in Friona.

However you took action, you need to shout your story from the rooftops—and from the water towers. Show your photos online, and in line at school, at the grocery store, anywhere. Tell kids. Tell adults. Tell everybody! Be sure to share with them the ways they can help, too.

Speak Up for Water

Water can't speak for itself. Neither can all the animals and plants that need clean, healthy water in oceans, lakes, rivers, and wetlands. So *you* can speak up for water. Here are some ideas:

- Put on a play. Act out the story of a seal pup in danger or a beaver dam being saved from destruction.

- Host a game show. Quiz the audience on water facts and ways they can save water.

- Compose a song or write a poem about your favorite water animal, your special water place, or the best part of the action you took.

- Write a short story about how you helped save and protect water. Get it published in a newspaper, magazine, or online, if you can.

- Send handmade thank-you cards to people who helped you on your service learning dive. They may want to be part of your next dive, too!

- Create a "Make a Splash" club and invite people to join. Together, come up with a list of things you'll do to protect water—close to home and around the world.

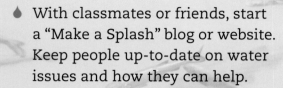

- With classmates or friends, start a "Make a Splash" blog or website. Keep people up-to-date on water issues and how they can help.

- Write an action-packed comic book about your exciting dive.

- Make a movie about water. Choose a subject that is important to you, whether it's clean drinking water, healthy coral reefs, or safe sea turtles.

- Write and direct a puppet show with a cast of watery characters. Make your puppets out of used items such as old socks or a wooden spoon. Will frogs give tips about saving water? Will sharks tell stories about living in the ocean?

- Design a "We Make a Splash!" certificate. Give it out to classrooms, restaurants, or shops that help water by recycling, using less electricity, or taking other actions.

- Write a letter to the editor of a newspaper. Share what you know about the threats facing water. Share your ideas about how people can help.

- Create a display or presentation of your action with photos and drawings. Make it big and splashy!

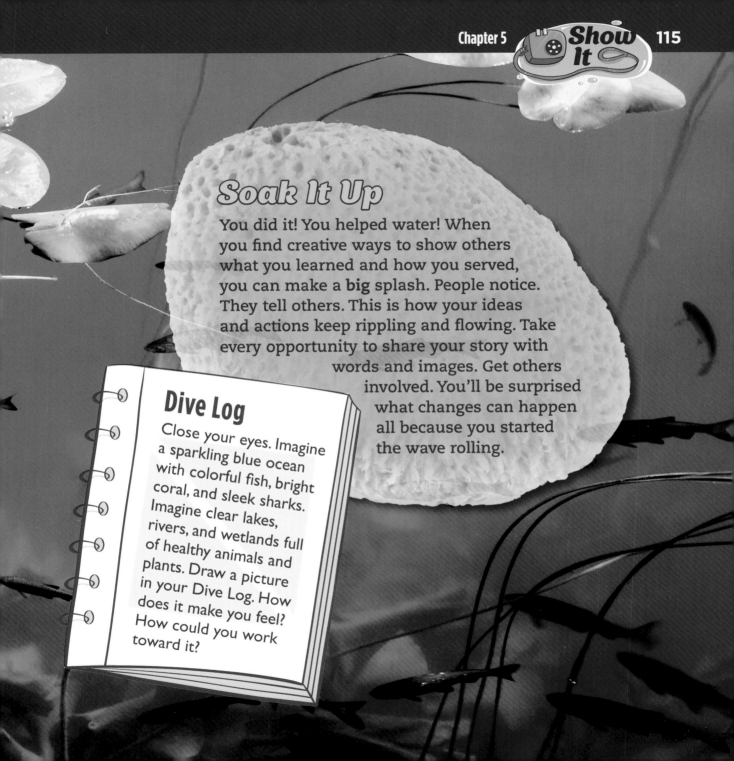

Soak It Up

You did it! You helped water! When you find creative ways to show others what you learned and how you served, you can make a **big** splash. People notice. They tell others. This is how your ideas and actions keep rippling and flowing. Take every opportunity to share your story with words and images. Get others involved. You'll be surprised what changes can happen all because you started the wave rolling.

Dive Log

Close your eyes. Imagine a sparkling blue ocean with colorful fish, bright coral, and sleek sharks. Imagine clear lakes, rivers, and wetlands full of healthy animals and plants. Draw a picture in your Dive Log. How does it make you feel? How could you work toward it?

What's Next?

Congratulations! You've taken your first big service learning dive.

You prepared.

You investigated.

You took action to help your water planet.

You reflected on what you did.

Then you told other people about water and how they could help, too.

And this is only the beginning. You still have your dive kit. Keep it handy and ready for use. Stay informed. Stay active. Use your knowledge, talents, and ideas to protect our oceans, lakes, rivers, and wetlands for years to come. And help others do the same.

EarthEcho Tip

Have you ever imagined being an explorer? Now is your chance. Our ocean is waiting for you. People have visited, photographed, mapped, and learned about nearly every part of our planet's land. However, most of our underwater world is still a mystery. Only 10 percent has been explored. Just think of all there is left to see! Your adventure with *Make a Splash!* is just a preview. The real story is how you *continue* to explore and care for water—from the water in your sink, to the water in the ocean. No matter if you live in the desert, on an ocean coast, or by a river, creek, pond, lake, or marsh ... water is all around you, and it needs your help now.

Our cofounder Phillipe's grandfather Jacques Cousteau said, "We protect what we love." We must protect this home we love, our water planet.

Words to Know

Advocacy: Giving voice to a serious problem or issue to promote solutions.

Aquifer: An underground layer of rock or soil that contains water.

Drought: Severe lack of rain in an area for a long time.

Estuary: A body of water, like a bay or lagoon, that forms near the mouth of a river.

Evaporate: To turn from liquid water into an invisible gas.

Food chain: The system of animals (including humans) using plants or other animals as a food source.

Glacier: A huge, slow-moving chunk of ice.

Greenhouse gases: Gases, like carbon dioxide and methane, which build up in the air and can make our planet warmer.

Phytoplankton: Tiny plants that live in the ocean and make oxygen.

Playa lakes: Temporary lakes that form only when it rains.

Reservoir: A human-made lake.

Scuba: Stands for "self-contained underwater breathing apparatus." Scuba gear allows people to breathe underwater and go on long dives.

Sediment: Sand, dirt, and gravel that sinks to the bottom of a body of water.

Upcycle: To take a used item and make it into something different, or to remake the same item how it used to be.

Water cycle: The continuous movement of water on, above, and below the surface of the earth.

Water table: Earth's supply of underground water.

Watershed: An area of land where all the water that is in it flows into the same place.

Waterway: Any body of water on Earth, such as a river, marsh, lake, sea, or ocean.

Wetlands: Wet places, like swamps and marshes, which store water as it slowly moves from one place to another.

Watery Websites and Bubbly Books

You are definitely not floating on your own out there. With a parent or teacher, visit these kid-friendly websites, and read the books, too. They have ideas, information, and examples of what *you* can do to make a splash.

Watery Websites

Discover Water is a website for kids by the Project WET Foundation. Learn all about the role of water in your life and how to use it wisely at discoverwater.org.

EarthEcho International is a group that empowers young people to take action to protect our water planet. EarthEcho inspires kids to make global change by meeting local needs. It also helps kids learn more about water issues. Go to earthecho.org and waterplanetchallenge.org.

Marine Animal Rehabilitation Center is part of a network of centers authorized by the National Marine Fisheries Service to nurse stranded marine mammals and sea turtles back to health. Visit une.edu/research/msc/marc and click on "Get Involved" to see how you can help these animals, too.

Monterey Bay Aquarium's website is full of amazing photos and videos and has a special section about how to take action to save our oceans. It's all at montereybayaquarium.org.

Roots & Shoots, founded by Dr. Jane Goodall, is dedicated to making positive change happen—for people, for animals, and for the environment. It helps thousands of kids in more than 120 countries join together to create a better world. Join them at rootsandshoots.org.

TerraCycle's purpose is to get rid of the idea of waste. They do this by creating national recycling systems for previously nonrecyclable or hard-to-recycle waste. Sign on by visiting their site at terracycle.com.

Bubbly Books

Ducky by Eve Bunting (Sandpiper, 2004). Are there really plastic bath toys floating in the ocean? This picture book is written from the perspective of one of the 28,800 ducks accidently released from a shipping container en route from Hong Kong to Seattle and lost at sea.

Flush by Carl Hiaasen (Yearling, 2010). Noah and his little sister, Abbey, dream up a crazy plan to stop a casino boat from polluting Florida's beaches—a plan so crazy that it just might work!

Gone Fishing: Ocean Life by the Numbers by David McLimans (Walker and Co., 2008). This counting book uses brilliant colors and the shapes of animals to count 1 to 10. Each animal represents sea life threatened by human activity. With information, statistics, and resources, this book has something for everyone.

Miss Fox's Class Goes Green by Eileen Spinelli (Albert Whitman & Company, 2011). When Miss Fox shows up at school riding her bicycle, Mouse asks, "Do you have a flat tire?" "No," Miss Fox tells her students. "I am going green!" Soon everyone in the class is working to keep the earth healthy.

Protecting Earth's Water Supply by Ron Fridell (Lerner Publications, 2008). Pollution and climate change are threatening our water supply. Read about creative solutions for collecting water and how a 10-year-old from India developed a water system to help local farmers.

Riparia's River by Michael Caduto (Tilbury House, 2010). When children find slime in their favorite swimming hole, they learn how the water became polluted. Together with the community, they come up with ideas to clean it up.

Splashy Sources

General

United States Environmental Protection Agency. (epa.gov)

Water.org. "Water Facts." (water.org/learn-about-the-water-crisis/facts)

Water Usage

U.S. Geological Society. "Water Science for Schools: Water Q & A: Water Use at Home." (ga.water.usgs.gov/edu/qahome.html)

Water Footprint Network. (waterfootprint.org)

Global Water Crisis

Human Development Report Office. "Human Development Report 2006: Beyond Scarcity: Power, Poverty and the Global Water Crisis." United Nations Development Programme.

Marks, Susan J. *Aqua Shock: The Water Crisis in America*. New York: Bloomburg Press, 2009.

Walsh, Bryan. "Parched Earth." *Time Magazine*. August 22, 2011.

Ocean Facts

The MarineBio Conservation Society. "Ocean Facts." (marinebio.org/MarineBio/Facts)

National Marine Sanctuaries. "Education." (sanctuaries.noaa.gov/education)

National Oceanic and Atmospheric Administration. "Ocean." United States Department of Commerce. (noaa.gov/ocean.html)

Ocean Conservancy, Inc. (oceanconservancy.org)

Office of Naval Research: Science & Technology Focus. "Oceanography." "Habitats." (onr.navy.mil/focus/ocean/habitats)

Save the Sea. "Interesting Ocean Facts." (savethesea.org/STS ocean_facts)

Climate Change

Chen, I-Ching, et al. "Rapid Range Shifts of Species Associated with High Levels of Climate Warming." *Science*, August 19, 2011: Vol. 333, no. 6045, pp. 1024–1026.

Suhr, Jim, and Steve Karnowski. "U.S. Drought 2012: Current Drought Covers Widest Area Since 1956, According to New Data." *Huffington Post*, July 16, 2012.

Pollution and Trash

Algalita Marine Research Institute. (algalita.org)

Basu, Saikat. "The Largest 'Landfill' on Earth; the Great Pacific Garbage Patch." *Digital Journal*. July 28, 2008.

CigaretteLitter.org. (cigarettelitter.org)

Ocean Conservancy, Inc. "Ten Things Kids Want to Know About Trash in the Ocean." (oceanconservancy.org/our-work/marine-debris/ten-things-kids-want-to-know.html)

Ocean Conservancy's International Coastal Cleanup. *Tracking Trash: 25 Years of Action for the Ocean: 2011 Report*. (coastal.ca.gov/publiced/ccd/coordinators/ICC_Marine_Debris_2011_Report.pdf)

Bottled Water

AllAboutWater.org. "The Effects of Bottled Water on the Environment." (allaboutwater.org/environment.html)

Royte, Elizabeth. *Bottlemania: Big Business, Local Springs, and the Battle Over America's Drinking Water*. New York: Bloomsbury Publishing, 2009.

Tappening. "Why Not Bottled Water?" (tappening.com/Why_Not_Bottled_Water)

The Container Recycling Institute. "Bottled Water." (container-recycling.org/issues/bottledwater.htm)

Index

A

Action ideas (Kids in Action)
  activities, 113–114
  biodiesel fuel from used
    cooking oil, 62
  cigarette butt planters, 89
  coral reef repair, 66
  lake awareness, 94
  playa festival, 85
  safe cleaning products, 58
  saving mangroves, 47
  saving water, 6, 37, 39, 42, 95
  stopping shark finning, 70–71
  trash cleanup, 90, 91
  trash prevention, 78, 82, 93
  tree planting, 45
  watershed study, 28
Action plan
  getting others involved, 96–97
  plan for, 100–102
  political involvement, 98–99
  spreading word about, 92,
    102–104
Animals
  bathing pets, 46
  climate change and, 63, 67–68
  oil spills and, 55–57, 87
  water needs of, 43–44
Anti-Bottle Project, 78
Aquifers, 15–16, 51, 85, 107, 111

B

Be Straw Free campaign, 93
Biodiesel fuel, 62

C

Camping, saving water when, 46
Carbon dioxide, 60, 61, 62
Cicada Tree Eco-Place, 47

Climate change
  about, 59–61
  animals and, 63, 67–68
  coral reefs and, 65
  lessening, 61–62
  melting ice from, 63, 67–68
  from methane, 79
  plants and, 63
Compost, 80
Conservation
  biodiesel fuel from used
    cooking oil, 62
  projects, 78, 82, 93
  recycling and upcycling, 79–82
  toys and, 76
  See also Saving water
Cooking oil, used, 62
Coral reefs, 53, 64–66, 69
Cousteau, Alexandra, 1, 5
Cousteau, Jacques-Yves, 2, 117
Cousteau, Philippe
  as boy, 1–2
  EarthEcho International, 5
  on Gulf of Mexico oil spill,
    55–56
  on responsible behavior, 52
Creeks, 24

D

Dive log, 12
  action projects, 95
  coral reefs, 64
  drinking water, 31
  going green and going blue,
    48
  Gulf oil spill, 57
  oceans recap, 83
  picture of healthy bodies of
    water, 115

  reflection, 108–109
  seabird protection, 73
  special water place, 4
  Team Water members, 99
  water treasure hunt, 22
  water use, 41
Drinking water, 29–30, 33
Drought, 16, 36

E

EarthEcho International, 5
Electricity, 41
Estuaries, 25
Evaporation, 19, 36

F

Farming and water use, 40
Faucets, leaky, 31
Fish, 25, 54, 69–71
Florida Keys, 66
Food and water use, 40
Food chains, 61
From the Tops of the Trees to the
  Bottom of the Pond, 28

G

Gagnan, Emile, 2
Glacier National Park, 63
Glaciers
  lakes and, 23
  melting, 63, 67–68
Going blue, 48
Going green, 48
Goodall, Jane, 82
Great Pacific Garbage Patch, 76
Greenhouse gases, 53, 60, 61, 65
Groundwater, 17, 36
Gulf of Mexico, 55–57

H

Home water use, 17, 38
Household cleaning products, 58
Human water needs, 32–33

L/M

Lakes, 23, 94
Landfills, 79
Litter, 87, 88–89
Mangroves, saving, 47
Methane, 79
Mobile Baykeeper, 58

O

Ocean coasts, 26, 54
Ocean Conservancy
        International Coastal
        Cleanup, 88
Oceans
    amount of Earth's water in, 33
    basins, 18–19
    climate change and, 59–61
    coral reefs in, 64–66
    melting, glaciers and, 63
    reasons for protecting, 52–54
    removing salt from, 35
    trash in, 53, 72–73, 76–77
    water sources for, 19
Ogallala Aquifer
    school project about, 51, 85,
        107, 111
    sources and uses, 15–16
Oil spills, 55–57, 87
Overfishing, 69
Oxygen, 53

P

Pets, bathing, 46
Phytoplankton, 53
Plants
    climate change and, 63
    water needs of, 17, 46

Plastic
    amount made, 75
    bottles, 77
    reusable bottles, 78
    shopping bags ban, 53, 82
    straws (drinking), 87, 93
    trash, 53, 75–76
Playa lakes, 15
Playa Posse, 85, 107, 111
Polar bears, 67
Political involvement, 98–99
Pollution, 36
    See also Trash
Power and water use, 41
Press releases, 103–104

R

Rainfall, 36
Recycling, 79–82
Reflection, 12, 108–109
Reusable Bag Campaign, 82
Reusable water bottles project,
        78
Ripple effect, 102–104
Rivers, 24
Roots & Shoots, 39, 71
Round Rock Elementary School,
        6

S

Salt water, 24
    See also all entries beginning
        with Ocean or Oceans
Save the Sharks Pledge
        Campaign, 71
Saving water
    action projects for, 6, 37, 39,
        42, 95
    bathing pets, 46
    camping, 44
    at home, 29, 31, 35, 39, 87, 91,
        94
    with toys, 76
Scuba, 2

Service learning, explained, 8–9
Shark finning, 70–71
Shellfish, 25, 54, 69
Stop Shark Finning Pledge
        Campaign, 70
Streams, 24

T

Team Water members, 98–99
Trash
    cleanup project ideas, 90, 91
    litter project, 89
    making zero waste, 74
    methane from, 79
    in oceans, 53, 72–73, 76–77
    plastic, 53, 75–76
    prevention project ideas, 78,
        82, 93
    recycling, 79–82
Turtles, 68, 69

U/V

Upcycling, 53, 80
Used Cooking Oil Recycling Act,
        62
Vapur Anti-Bottles, 78

W

Water cycle, 19–20
Water Drops: Message to
        Humanity, 37
Water facts, 17–18
Watersheds, 22, 27–29
Water supply, 33, 36
Water use
    average by country, 34
    by business, 17
    for different purposes at
        home, 17, 38
    for food, 40
    for power, 41
    See also Saving water
Wetlands, 7, 24–25

About the Authors

Cathryn Berger Kaye, M.A., is an international service learning and education consultant and former classroom teacher. She presents at conferences around the world and works with students, teachers, schools, and state departments. While Cathy has lived in many places and enjoys traveling, she is glad to feel the ocean breezes at her home in Los Angeles. Most of all, she adores her family—husband Barry and two daughters, Ariel and Devora—who inspire her daily. Cathy's books include *Going Blue: A Teen Guide to Saving Our Oceans, Lakes, Rivers, & Wetlands* (with Philippe Cousteau), *The Complete Guide to Service Learning*, and the How to Take Action! series of student workbooks.

Philippe Cousteau is an explorer, social entrepreneur, and environmental advocate. He is the grandson of the legendary Captain Jacques Cousteau—the man who invented scuba diving and introduced the world to life under the sea. Philippe and his sister, Alexandra, started EarthEcho International, a leading nonprofit environmental education organization. He also created the Global Echo Foundation, which aims to help solve many of the world's challenges. Philippe serves as a special correspondent for CNN International, has written for *National Geographic*, and has testified before Congress on issues facing our oceans.

Email the authors at help4kids@freespirit.com.

Teachers, youth leaders, parents, and other adults:
Download the free online Leader's Guide at freespirit.com/splash.
